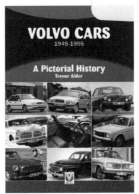

www.veloce.co.uk

First published in April 2024 by Veloce, an imprint of David and Charles Limited. Tel +44 (0)1305 260068 / e-mail info@veloce.
co.uk / web www.veloce.co.uk.
ISBN: 978-1-845846-13-8; UPC: 6-36847-04613-2.

VOLVO CARS

1945-1995

A Pictorial History
Trevor Alder

VELOCE

CONTENTS

INTRODUCTION

Volvo cars were certainly not mainstream in the UK until perhaps the late 1960s, but gradually earned a reputation for being reliable, solid and dependable. My association with anything Volvo started in 1977 with my father's 1972 metallic gold 145E, a high mileage quirky car with gearbox whine and a splendid Webasto fold-back full-length sun roof. I was lucky enough to be in the Under Seventeen Car Club, and after a vetting of my driving skills by Tony Dron (ex-editor of *Classic Cars* magazine) I was permitted to drive, along with other teenagers in their parents' cars, on half of a closed Silverstone racing circuit in that very 145E. Fond memories of speeding down Hanger Straight at over 70mph at such a young age still make me smile ...

Having taken my driving test in the 145E in 1979 whilst still in sixth form, I was amazed that I passed first time, and also by the fact that my father let me loose in it with a few school friends, seven up, driving the Essex countryside after a new Chelmsford

Asda store sold petrol on special offer of just 75 pence per gallon (or 16 pence per litre). Those days are long gone, but since then I have been happy to own a number of Volvos, including an early 1967 144, a 245, a 480 ES and a 1990 240 GL estate, and I enjoyed every one of them, including the somewhat erratic electrics on the 480, which sadly was destined for the local scrap yard in 2003 ...

Moving to Ipswich in the mid-1980s, the local docks were crammed full of new Volvos fresh off the boat from Sweden, with Volvo Concessionaires issuing all press cars with local Suffolk registrations, and their transportation through Ipswich town commonplace. The ex-Volvo buildings still stand today, long since abandoned as the operational HQ moved further west in the 1990s.

This book chronicles the postwar UK Volvo car scene up to around 1995, and includes references to those models that also became available only for overseas markets. It does not aim to cover any heavier commercial Volvos, although there is a brief appendix on military applications

The author and his father in 2018 at a Suffolk classic car event.

and car-based vans. Throughout the main chapters, in blue tinted boxes, there are a variety of the headlines used in contemporary advertising from various sources, including some from overseas. These are certainly not exhaustive (there truly are hundreds for certain models), but I have tried to include every model manufactured. Many headlines used are tongue in cheek, including a 1986 double page spread for the 740 Turbo estate in which it was claimed "The only souped-up car that can carry 3988 cans of soup ..." This had the copywriters' wrists slapped, as the UK Advertising Standards Authority stated "though capable of holding the cans, the 740 estate could not be driven with such a load." The weight of those cans, shown stacked seven deep to the roof, would have been around 3500lb (1600kg), way more than the permitted legal amount! Of course in reality, those familiar 'stack of Volvos' adverts clearly show a bottom car capable of withstanding a massive load: ironically, the 740 estate shown at the bottom of the stack does look like it's about to burst, with around seven and a half tons of Volvos carefully craned into position on top of it.

The book is divided into logical chapters, and within these included are specific model histories, key (but not all) production changes, a brief overview of specifications and performance, and a whole variety of photographs, many of them period, that hopefully serve as a useful guide to the manufacturer that utilised so many British parts of vehicles often built all over the world. The production figures proved interesting to research; it must be pointed out that the 1950-1968 build figures previously published were often rounded seemingly up or down, and usually ended in a zero or two for each year for specific models. Nigh on impossible, of course!

Thanks to Kevin Price (Volvo Enthusiasts' Club) for his help and hospitality, Volvo cars for use of some of the photos, and the many owners and enthusiasts to whom I have spoken.

The Volvo museum at Gothenburg and Daf museum in Holland are certainly worth mentioning for a visit, featuring a number of very interesting exhibits, both cars and trucks.

Trevor Alder
Ipswich, UK

"Once you've seen how much they cost, check how long they last" (1978 UK advertisement)

Line drawings copyright Trevor Alder, 2023.

This book is dedicated to my mother, Jean.
April 1938–April 2023

PV444 & PV544

The PV444 design was finalised as early as 1944, and soon after this the PV53-57 prewar passenger car range was phased out. The PV444 was Volvo's first truly mass produced car, with a somewhat homely looking bodywork of unitary construction, modern coil spring suspension, a laminated safety windscreen, three-speed synchromesh gearbox and 1.6-litre engine. Produced alongside it were the larger low production PV60 (1946-50) and PV82 (1947-48) models, which sold in hundreds rather than thousands. In 1947, PV444 production commenced and the car came in a strong two-door form only, with total sales around 12,500 by 1950. 17 per cent of the PV's components were manufactured in the UK, including the brakes. The original, rather unusual metal and plastic dashboard was replaced in 1951, with other internal improvements made.

Two years later (PV445) three-door vans, estates and a pick-up started to trickle off the production lines, using a separate ladder chassis. Italian coachbuilder Michelotti designed the elegant Elizabeth I built on a PV445 chassis. The PV was of American style, similar to contemporary Chevrolets and Cadillacs, but had much smaller European dimensions, being a compact 14ft 9in long and 5ft 2in wide. All models produced were left-hand drive (Sweden not converting to driving on the right until 1967) and were built domestically in Lundby, until production commenced in Brazil and Canada. A major and noticeable production change was the adoption of a larger one-piece rear window and higher front windscreen in 1954.

Research for this book reveals that the weekly UK motoring press, despite having hardly any official imports, tested the PV444 seven times, mainly with the 1414cc engine and usually in Sweden. When a 1.4-litre PV444 Swedish-registered car was first tested by *The Motor* magazine in March 1950, it attained a top speed of 74.1mph, 0-60mph acceleration in 24.9 seconds and average economy of around 33mpg, which the magazine described back then as "brisk performance." Moving forwards seven years with the same magazine

An early PV444 van, popular with Swedish utility companies.

The original 1947-1951 style metal dashboard with plastic surrounds.

A PV444 of around 1955 vintage. This model has just received the one-piece rear window, but retained the split front windscreen.

and test format, and the figures improved for the 1.6-litre PV444L of the same weight and dimensions (the 16in wheels now 15in): top speed was now 94.1mph, 0-60mph in 14.5 seconds and an average economy of 26.8mpg. *Autocar* tested a PV444 with a 'sports engine' (again rated at 85bhp) which was very slightly lower in performance. No later Duetts were ever tested in the UK.

An early PV interior. Access to the rear compartment was certainly good. The PV444 was strictly a four-seater; the PV544 was a five-seater by redesigning the rear seat.

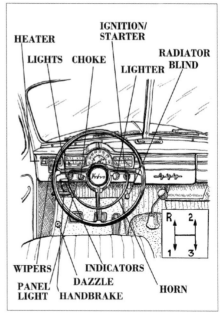

Second type of dashboard, 1955 designation.

After nine years of PV production, Volvo took its first stand at the 1956 Motor Show in London, and this was the only time a PV was exhibited with a UK price tag. The PV444 appeared in the UK new car price lists for just a year until November 1957, last listed at £1100. A Volvo show stand was also taken in London in 1958 but there was a noticeable absence of any PVs – including the new 544 - concentration of course was on the new Amazon P120 and soon after, the sporty P1800. The PV444 appeared in the UK new car price lists for just a year until November 1957, last listed at £1100. The rectangular grille was fitted from 1956, and the California model had twin carbs increasing power from 51 to 70hp.

In autumn 1958, the aforementioned 95hp PV544 was introduced. At first glance it was very similar with mainly the same panels, but this model utilised the curved glass technology popular in the car industry throughout the 1950s, and featured a one-piece windscreen replacing the raked V-screen of the 444. For some models there was a four-speed gearbox and the front grille

This PV444 was driven 4000 miles from Vancouver to Halifax as a publicity stunt.

9

A P210 Duett poses at the Volvo Enthusiasts' Club rally in 2022 as a more modern 850 estate passes by.

This PV544 was first imported to the UK in 1991, and photographed at the turn of the millennium. The PV544 is quickly identified by its single-piece front windscreen.

The same P210 has masses more load capacity than its PV544 sister saloon car. Note the 12 wooden slats on the cargo area floor and back seat.

Rear aspect of the same PV544. This larger rear screen replaced the two-piece unit from 1954 on the PV444.

was bigger and of more modern appearance, whilst the rear lamp clusters were somewhat larger than the 444 model's. Internally, there was now a ribbon-style speedometer, and the rear passenger seat was revised to make it a true five-seater. In autumn 1960, the newly designated P210 replaced the commercial PV445 platform that had been running alongside. This now took the single front screen on the PV544 saloon, and lost its swage line on the sides over the rear axle. There were also ambulance and other commercial versions. By 1962 the vehicle electrics were upgraded from 6 to 12 volts. The PV544 had international success in rallying, but surprisingly did not capitalise on this through media advertising. Despite the inception of the new P120 in 1957, sales still increased with over 100,000 units sold from 1958 to 1960.

Dashboard arrangement of the same 1779cc 1965 P210 car.

Saloon (always two-door) production continued until 1965, including in North America at the new Halifax facility from June 1963, and the P210 utility models battled on until 1969 (in Brazil with a lower roof line and split tailgate like the Amazon estate), with over half a million produced on all platforms.

The speedometer of the P210, inherited from the PV544.

PV media advertising slogans

A product of superb Swedish engineering (PV444 brochure)

We can't say how long a used Volvo will last. We've only been making them 68 years (PV544 and 460 in 1995)

... for agility and economy (USA, PV444)

Volvo is the car with Speed, Economy, Comfort, Service, Appeal (USA Duett and PV444)

The car with the sparkling performance (PV444 brochure)

Swedish excellence for practical Americans (PV444 USA)

See it, drive it, you will buy it (USA PV544)

Swedish cars of class with speed to spare (PV544 and Amazon)

It's a family car! It's a sports car! (USA PV544)

Farewell old friend (USA PV544)

Volvo is the sports car, family style (PV544)

Economy does not mean compromise (USA PV544)

Miles later, years later, you'll still be glad you bought a Volvo! (1960 PV544 and Amazon)

PV BODY TYPES: two-door saloon (PV444) and two-door Duett (PV445 estate, pick-up, cabriolet or van) from 1953; **manufactured at**: Lundby (Sweden), Carbrasa – Rio de Janeiro (Brazil), Halifax (Canada) from 1963; **number produced**: 196,005 (PV444), 4030 (PV445), 12,394 (PV445 pick-up), 9126 (PV445 Duett), 3859 (PV445 van), 243,995 (PV544/P110), 60,959 (P210), total PV 530,368; **production span**: 1947-1965 (Duett extended to 1968).

PERFORMANCE: top speed (saloons): 85-90mph/135-145kph; **0-60mph/100kph**: 19-25 sec; **average economy**: 25-33mpg.

PRICE AT LAUNCH: £1100 (PV444 UK in 1956).

MEASUREMENTS: **length**: (PV444) 14ft 9in (4.5m), Duett 14ft 5¼in (4.4m); **width**: 5ft 2in (1.57m); **height**: 5ft 1½in (1.56m), Duett 5ft 7in (1.7m); **wheelbase**: 8ft 6½in (2.6m); **weight**: 2128lb (965kg) saloon; **wheels**: 16/15in; **turning circle**: 33ft 6in (10.2m); **fuel capacity**: 7¾ gallons/35 litres (saloon); **boot footprint**: 40 x 42in (saloon); **boot load height**: 18½in.

TECHNICAL: **engine types**: 1414, 1580, 1778cc, all four-cyl. petrol; **gearbox**: three-speed manual, four-speed optional; **suspension**: (front) wishbones/coil, (rear) coil (but leaf springs on Duett); **brakes**: drum hydraulic front and drum rear.

TRIM: vinyl leathercloth, two-tone cloth.

KEY OPTIONAL EXTRAS: four-speed manual transmission.

This splendid large-scale model of the PV displays its 'beetle-back' appearance very well.

AMAZON SERIES

The announcement of the 'Amason' to the existing dealer base was in February 1956, joining the long-standing PV444 cars, but factory production started a year later. The all-new Volvo was a more modern car, with a longer wheelbase and wider track courtesy of young chief design engineer, 26-year-old Jan Wilsgaard. It had a strong resemblance to the European Borgward and Peugeot 403. Kreidler, a manufacturer that held about one third of the German sales of motorcycles, located near Stuttgart, Germany, raised concerns about the name, claiming it held the trademark (its Amazone moped was produced between 1956-1958), so when exports started, Volvo adopted numerical names, the Amazon moniker only appearing in Sweden after some negotiation.

Early September 1956 saw the first domestic showing of some pre-production Amazons at a show at Orebro, Sweden, 170 miles north east of Gothenburg, and hundreds of 4000 kronor deposits (total price then was 12,600 knonor) were taken from an eager Swedish public, with deliveries to occur five months later. Seven weeks later, with a humble stand at the back of the main hall, furthest from the public entrance and hiding behind the various Rolls-Royce models, Volvo exhibited for the first ever time at a UK Motor Show, in Earl's Court, London following its stand at the recent Paris show earlier that month. On display was a new 1.6-litre single carburettor two-tone Amazon with a 6-volt power system and just 60hp but, for the first time for a Volvo, four doors. It was available in four two-tone colour schemes. Details were also made available of a special export model called the Californian. Also on show here were the PV444 and the short-lived plastic-bodied sports convertible, about to be upgraded from a three-speed to a five-speed gearbox.

After skipping the 1957 UK Motor Show, a solitary 122S (note new name) was on display at the October 1958 event, following its debut throughout European shows that year with the more powerful B16B 85hp engine and whitewall tyres. The same albeit enlarged theme continued in 1959 when Volvo was

Amazon in the mid-1950s in New York city. This stunning strawberry and cream colour scheme proved very popular.

An 85hp 122S visits the zoo; some early press photography.

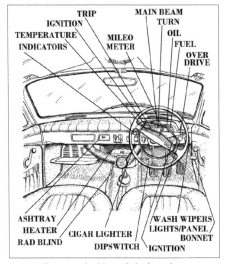

TRIP
IGNITION
TEMPERATURE
INDICATORS
MILEO
METER
MAIN BEAM
TURN
OIL
FUEL
OVER
DRIVE

ASHTRAY
HEATER
RAD BLIND
CIGAR LIGHTER
DIPSWITCH
WASH WIPERS
LIGHTS/PANEL
BONNET
IGNITION

Amazon dashboard designation.

The 121 two-door saloon. A122S in blue was displayed at the 1959 London Motor Show complete with perspex bonnet and boot lid. A cutaway engine exhibit was also on display.

An early GT prepares for some fast driving.

sandwiched between the Lotus and Simca stands with three two-tone 122S cars and a cutaway engine exhibit. Britain was never to see the B16A 60hp Amazon that was exhibited in 1957; indeed, it wasn't until 1959 that UK journalists were able to drive a Volvo, due to complete non-availability.

Production cranked up (after just over 5000 cars were built in the first two years), and 1959 also saw the 122S launched in the USA at the New York Automotive show. 1960 saw gearbox changes and the availability of electric Laycock overdrive. The model continued until 1964 in standard form, but a more powerful front-disc braked B18 derivative arrived in late 1961 and lasted until the end of 1967; at the same time two-tone paintwork

was deleted. The £1372 122S B18 had a 115mph calibrated speedometer, sported a red B18 badge on its revised wider mesh radiator grille and rear boot lid, and a highly polished B18 engine was displayed at the various Motor Shows. The two-door 121 made its debut in March 1962 and continued for four years. By summertime, reversing lamps were fitted as standard across the range.

A five-door shooting brake version with the B18 engine arrived in February 1962, with the first public display of two pale green examples (the only colour available) to a home audience at the 200-car Stockholm Motor Show, the UK seeing earliest deliveries by the end of the year. It had fold-flat rear seats revealing six feet of usable cargo length, a pop-up rear

The Amazon estate was sold from February 1962, with UK models taking a few months to arrive.

The Amazon estate was 14ft 7in long – 8in shorter than its successor, the 145.

window that opened when the lower tailgate was lowered (a gas strut followed two years later), and it shared the same length and wheelbase as the saloons. The number plate hinged downward when load-carrying, like the 1959 Mini, and copied by the 1970 Range Rover, which also shared the horizontally split tailgate theme. A handy step was utilised on the rear bumper for when an optional roof rack was fitted.

The somewhat taller PV544 Duett was to continue alongside for some time. The 221 badge arrived later, in October 1965, with it known just as the estate until then, and it was produced until the inception of the new 145 in 1968. A 223 GT estate lasted just a year from November 1967.

The 100,000th Amazon was built in February 1963, and three months later Prince Bertil of Sweden opened the Nova Scotia production facility in Canada for the North American market. By the autumn of 1963, the boot handle incorporated the number plate light. The UK began receiving more estate cars for local delivery, and, due to excise duty changes by the EFTA (European Free Trade Area), new car prices were reduced accordingly. The summer of 1964 saw an upholstery change: textile-reinforced vinyl fabric on orthopaedic seats with variable lumber support control were introduced, and, in September, a black Amazon two-door became the millionth Volvo to be built. October 1964 saw the first of the twin-carburettor 75hp 131 'coupés' (a single carburettor version was available too), essentially a two-

An Amazon P220 estate with PV544 Duett.

The later safety dished steering wheel of 1968. This was shared with the 140 series.

The split, horizontally-folding tailgate arrangement of the Amazon estate, photographed in 2022.

A B22 engine 122S with stylish Minilite alloy wheels alongside a P210.

B20 engine power in the Amazon, which was capable of 105mph.

Engine bay of 1.8-litre 1968 122S.

A well looked after interior of a 122S.

A 1966 121S at a Suffolk car show in 2022.

Front seats of the 122S.

door model that lasted until end of production in 1970. New for 1966 season was the hottish 122S twin carburettor saloon, raise in compression ratio to 8.7:1, from 90 to 95bhp.

The similar looking, short-lived, 132S 95hp coupé ran for two years from November 1965, and at this point an economy three-speed Amazon Favorite was offered with black paint, a red interior and very minimal trim. Automatic cars with the Borg-Warner Type 35 transmission joined the range in summer

An immaculate 122S two-door poses with a P1800.

A pair of white 122S cars.

Front aspect of a 1968 1.8-litre 131.

1966, identified by an alloy badge on the boot lid. To add to a confusing set of model numbers, further short-lived models were the 133 (100hp) and powerful 105mph 123 GT based on the 130 two-door platform, initially 1.8-litre but alongside the P1800, with later models offered as 2-litre (115hp). The 123 GT adopted the P1800 steering wheel, featured new wheel trims, a rev counter, fog and spot lamps. Both 133 and 123 GT were November 1967-1969. Late 1967 cars saw a split steering column that collapsed in the event of a heavy accident, and by the end of the year the four-door saloon production halted giving way to the new 144 cars.

The B20 2-litre was fitted from August 1968 (B20A 90hp, B20B 118hp). The P220 estate bailed out in summer 1969, leaving a somewhat rationalised Amazon range that was now fitted with headrests and rear seat belts as standard. The last Amazon style car was built in Torslanda on 3rd July 1970. Over two thirds of a million were produced by the factory overall, with just over 19,000 in the last model

Rear aspect of the 1968 1.8-litre 131.

Chrome detailing of some Amazon cars. The door mirror features the original Volvo motif. Confusingly, badges always state 121 or 122.

The Amazon always had openings for two grilles behind the metalwork, whatever age the car. The grilles themselves differed slightly between models.

year. According to SMMT figures, the last 27 of the UK designated P130 cars were registered in the second half of 1971.

The Ruddspeed Amazons

Known for dealing in Aston Martins, Rudds of Worthing, UK, produced the rally inspired Ruddspeed Amazon in two-door, four-door and even estate form, and also tuned the P1800S. All Q-car style models boasted sports car acceleration and handling characteristics, with fitted dual twin choke Weber carburettors, increased sound

proofing, front Girling disc brakes, suspension modifications and carpeting, and promised to overtake many cars that Volvos had never passed before ... Price was an all-in £1195 in 1965, and the local West Sussex Police Constabulary was persuaded to purchase a Ruddspeed 131 model with special hand-polished cylinder head, four-branch exhaust, alternator, Koni dampers, wider wheels and several other modifications. As the speedometer often over-read by 20 per cent, at the top speed of 102mph it would have been showing nearly 125mph – hopefully the boys in blue had their own correct calibration on board! A *Country Life* road test of the estate version remarked "Initial experience with the car in town driving was most encouraging. It gives the impression of

being a standard 3-litre rather than a tuned 2-litre car, because so much normal driving can be done in top gear ..." and "... full use of the gearbox converts the car into a close resemblance to a fierce sports car."

AMAZON BODY TYPES: P120 four-door saloon, P130 two-door coupé, P220 five-door estate; **manufactured at:** Lundby, then Torslandaverkan, Gothenburg from April 1964 (Sweden), Ghent (Belgium), Halifax (Canada), Durban (South Africa), Arica (Northern Chile); **approximate number produced:** 234,208 (P120 four-door), 359,918 (P130 two-door), 73,197 (P220 estate), totalling 667,323; **production span:** 1957-1970.
PERFORMANCE: top speed: 85-105mph/140-170kph; **0-60mph/100kph:** 14-18 seconds (B20 2-litre 10.2 sec); **average economy:** 23-28mpg.
PRICE AT LAUNCH: 12,600 Kronor, £868 (approx) in 1958.
MEASUREMENTS: length: 14ft 7¼in (4.45m); **width:** 5ft 3¾in (1.61m); **height:** 4ft 11½in (1.51m); **wheelbase:** 8ft 6½in (2.6m); **weight:** (saloon) 2324lb (1056kg), (estate) 2586lb (1173kg); **wheels:** 15in; **turning circle:** 32ft 6in (9.9m); **fuel capacity:** 10 gallons/45 litres; **boot capacity:** 12ft^3 (approx., saloon), 65ft^3 (estate with seats down, 72in length).
TECHNICAL: engine types: 1583, 1778, then (B20) 1986cc from 1968, all four-cyl. petrol; **gearbox:** early cars are three- then four-speed manual (either with overdrive option), Borg Warner automatic and overdrive; **suspension:** (front) independent coil springs and wishbones, (rear) live axle, coil springs; **brakes:** drum then disc front and drum rear, later models had rear disc, servo unit on estate.
TRIM: Cloth, vinyl, leather.
KEY OPTIONAL EXTRAS: Overdrive, estate roof rack with bumper step for access.

P1800 SERIES

During 1956-57, Volvo learned the hard way that launching and selling a new sports car was certainly not straightforward. The Volvo Sport, or P1900, sold only 67 units and was about as near as you could get to a predecessor to the P1800. A convertible of high quality fibreglass construction, it was around 4in shorter and narrower than the forthcoming P1800, and was powered by the then current PV's 70hp 1414cc engine. Despite weighing just 970kg, performance was not its strong point. For promotion, it was displayed at various motor shows, including London in 1956, with eager plans to update it with a five-speed gearbox. Even now it has a strong following in enthusiast circles.

May 1959 saw some interesting press photographs of the all-new 1800, with motoring magazine headlines like "British bodywork for a Volvo sports coupé," claiming that its manufacture would be under way by the end of the year at the Pressed Steel Company in Linwood, Scotland (production was at its limit in the Swedish plants with the PV544 and Amazon models). Paintwork and trimming was to be performed by Jensen Motors in the UK Midlands in a new factory near Birmingham.

In reality, this scenario would happen much later, but in January 1960 a single P958-X1 1800 prototype (essentially a pre-production P1800) was displayed in public for the first time at the Brussels Motor Show in Belgium. Its original 1957 design stood well, with little change, although the rear styling was reworked a little, and it was announced that a new four-cylinder 1780cc engine would power this new coupé, with four-speed all synchromesh gearing taken from the 122S.

Non-production novelties were: an attractive 'V' motif on the front grille, opening rear quarter windows, and front and rear matching bumpers – a two-part cow-horn style, with the twin exhausts leaving through tailored rear panel port holes. Rally driver Pat Moss was reported to have commented on the new car at the 1960 October UK Motor Show, stating that she even preferred the P1800 over the stylish new Alfa Romeo Giulietta.

The UK was a good choice for initial manufacture, after considering other potential plants at Holland, Germany and Belgium. Indeed, many of the car's components were already UK sourced: Sankey wheels, Girling disc brakes for the front, Pirelli Centura tyres, Wilmot-Breeden door locks, Smiths instrumentation, Triplex glass, Hardy Spicer propeller shafts, Laycock-de Normanville overdrive, SU carburettors and various Lucas electrical items. Initially all cars were left-hand drive, with the first UK right-hand drive built in July 1961, and completed vehicles were ferried back to Sweden for quality checks before being signed off for onward delivery.

A forerunner to the P1800? The fibreglass bodied Volvo P1900 Sports convertible was a brave and expensive move into the cabriolet market. Just 67 were built in 1956, and it shared its engine with the PV series.

Front aspect of a very early Jensen-built P1800 in 2022. Note early all-white indicator covers and 'Cow Horn' bumpers.

Rear aspect of the same immaculate car displays the red-only rear lamps and correct optional mudflaps.

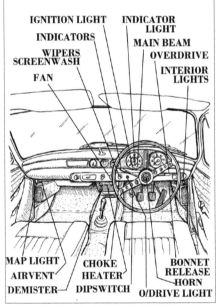

Earliest dashboard designation.

An early Jensen car's red rear lamp cluster, a later 1800S boot badge, rear safety belt hanging point, and distinctive Volvo badge mounted on the 'C' pillar, which featured on only the earliest Jensen-built cars.

Interior and dashboard of the 1962 P1800.

An early production car was shown at the Geneva Motor Show in early 1961, a platform that was also used by Jaguar to launch its E-Type sports roadster, and in mid-1961 the motoring press headlines stated "production in Britain." Throughout 1961, the P1800 was always centre stage at the motor shows. In March 1962, seven of the first right-hand drive cars were signed off to dealers for demonstration at a special ceremony near London. The earliest and Jensen-built models had white front indicators, all-red rear lights and a special badge on the 'C' post.

Production in the UK continued until early 1963 and around 6000 cars, when it was moved to Lundby factory in Sweden (the 'S' designation stood for Sverige/Sweden). A 'hot'

The rear seating of the P1800 could best be described as limited! Note the matching colour safety belts.

A peek through the steering wheel reveals the rev counter and speedometer.

The four-cylinder 1769cc engine.

Ten years separate this later model 144 and 1800. New Yorker Irv Gordon drove 3¼ million miles before his death in 2018, and his car (not the 1800 photographed) became the highest mileage private vehicle driven by the original owner in non-commercial service.

camshaft, harder valve springs and raised compression ratio occurred in August 1963 which also saw slightly revised instrumentation and internal door trim, new bucket and occasional rear seats, and new pressed steel wheels with hub caps. The cow-horn front bumper was replaced with a straight unit with a rubber strip, which was also added to

the rear one. Front turn indicators now went orange, and by now the 1962-1967 thriller TV series The Saint was airing, which helped sales tremendously. By 1964, Ruddspeed was

Minilite wheels and all the correct chrome ...

in on the tuning act, its adverts claiming extra power, along with its Amazon offerings.

From very late 1965, a shinier front grille replaced the earlier unit. A C-type camshaft fitted boosted power to 115bhp, and a rear brake limiting valve was fitted. The P1800 was now a 'greased for life' car as grease nipples on the steering gear and propeller shaft were eliminated. August 1966 saw the double-line front grille arrive, and a straight chrome side strip soon replaced the earlier upwards tick complimenting new style door handles. July 1967 saw the padded three-spoke steering wheel and burst-proof door locks introduced, plus revised ashtray and internal door handles. Just over a year later came the 118hp B20 2-litre motor, and to identify this such models had a B20 badge placed on the front grille. Further modifications were dual-circuit brakes and a sealed cooling system. Despite now being a 2-litre, it was still called the P1800.

By late 1969 the 1800E had been announced with Bosch electronic fuel-injection (better for the strict US emissions), a revised camshaft (now 135bhp) and all-round disc brakes. 'Clover Rim' wheels were now featured, as were a matt black grille. Ventilation

The chrome trim on the sides swept up along with the door swage line until the mid-1960s, when it became fully horizontal.

New Yorker Irv Gordon drove this P1800 3¼ million miles before his death in 2018: his car became the highest mileage private vehicle driven by the original owner in non-commercial service. (Courtesy Volvo)

One of the last 1800E cars built, a rarely seen convertible model in Suffolk in 2022. Harold Radford built two convertibles for a Hull dealer in the early 1960s, and around 50 conversions are reported to have been made by US dealer Volvoville.

Cutaway illustration of the 1971-73 1800 ES. Top speed was around 110mph.

Rear aspect of the 1800 ES. The rear tailgate was frameless.

This 1800 ES photo dates to around 1972, when the 140 and 160 series were offered in the same white gold metallic colour.

was improved, most noticeably by the new pronounced fresh air vents fitted to the rear wings, and the fuel filler was relocated to the left rear side panel. There was a revised dashboard with brand new dials and imitation wood fascia. Not available for six months on the UK market until March 1970 (the P1800 was noted by its absence at the 1969 London show), *Motor* magazine soon road tested an example and attained 112mph top speed, with a 0-60mph time of just 9.5 seconds. The Laycock electric overdrive option was intended to operate in top gear only. Automatic became an option for this engine from September 1970 but was rarely fitted. August 1971

saw a black plastic grille and revised steel wheels fitted, plus updated badging, door trims and inertia reel safety belts. There were redesigned, much plusher and thicker seats with integral headrests. Overall, 9414 1800E cars were built before June 1972, when production ceased.

The striking 1800 ES 'sporting estate' was first seen at the October 1971 Paris Motor Show as the Volvo Viking 2+2, competing for a similar audience to the Reliant Scimitar GTE customer base. Compared to the 1800 coupé it was 4in longer, around 200lb heavier (but on the same wheelbase) but just 2mph slower on top speed. Dubbed the 'Beach Car,'

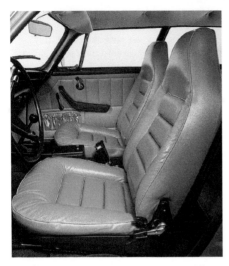

This 1973 1800 ES sold for a record-breaking $92,400 at a Bonhams auction in 2014. It had covered just under 13,000 miles.

A very late 1800 ES with the extremely comfortable last run leather seats and integral head restraints. Note lumbar support. The last price listed in the UK was £3042 (overdrive) or £3089 (automatic) in October 1973.

A US specification 1800 ES with optional chrome roof rack; just right for those skiing trips ...

Outside the Volvo museum in Sweden, 47 P1800s gather for a photo shoot. All were from Swiss and German clubs. Overall, 80 per cent of 1800 production was sent to Canada/USA.

but scornfully referred to as the 'Fiskbilen' (Swedish for 'fish van'), the 1800 ES had a frameless all-glass tailgate, a design also carried across to the later 1980s 480 and 1990s C3 cars. Rearward visibility was much improved.

Three design concepts had been built for the ES, and one of the two Italian ones (by Frua) is still in the Volvo museum. The final approved design was by in-house designers Jan Wilsgaard and Pelle Petterson. A rare car, some 8077 ES models were built in two years. P1800 ES production stopped on 27th June 1973, and the last P1800 model year saw just the ES being manufactured, having seen over 39,000 coupés over an 11-year period. The production facility was then reconfigured to make way for the C300 off-road vehicle from 1974.

Final all-model modifications included new side impact protection, halogen headlamps, and all interior materials were made fire resistant during summer of 1972. The first gear ratio was lowered for better take-off when fully laden, and new colours were offered. Finally there were dashboard switchgear changes, and the wipers swept 10 per cent more of the windscreen.

1800 media advertising slogans
Driving isn't bad for it (1800S 1968 USA)
Behaves like an angel... goes like the devil (1800S)
This is either the most expensive economy car in the world, or the least expensive Gran Turismo car in the world. We'll sell you either one (1800S, USA)
This car is 44mph slower than the rest of the cars in its class. It's also $6000 cheaper (1800S, USA)
Volvo introduces a sports car that really hauls (1800 ES, USA)
What's it like to drive a $10,000 car? Find out for $3995 (1800S, USA)
He never dreamed his $4150 investment would make a million
In a class by itself (USA 1963 P1800)
It's sort of a souped down Ferrari (1800S)
It goes faster without the carburetors (USA 1800E)
Volvo's E-Type (USA 1800E)

1800 BODY TYPES: two-door coupé, three-door sporting estate; **manufactured at**: Linwood, Scotland (panels) then assembly in West Bromwich (UK) until 1963, then Lundby/Gothenburg/Torslanda (Sweden), and CKD assembly in Arica (Chile); **number produced**: 30,407 coupé, and 8077 (ES); **production span**: 1961-1973.

PERFORMANCE: **top speed**: 105mph/170kph (carb), 112mph/180kph (fuel injected 2-litre); **0-60mph/100kph**: 12.5 sec (carb), or 9.6 sec (fuel injected 2-litre); **average economy**: 32mpg (carb), 25mpg (fuel injected).

PRICE AT LAUNCH: £1858 (1962 coupé), £2651 (1971 ES).

MEASUREMENTS: **length**: 14ft 2½in (4.33m) (coupé), 14ft 6¼in (4.43m) (ES); **width**: 5ft 6½in (1.69m); **height**: 4ft 2½in (1.28m); **wheelbase**: 8ft ½in (2.45m); **weight**: 2383lb (1085kg) (coupé), 2585lb (1177kg) (ES); **wheels**: 15in; **turning circle**: 31ft (9.44m); **fuel capacity**: 10 gallons/45 litres; **boot capacity**: 8.1ft^3 (coupé), boot floor length (with seats down) 5ft (1.5m) and 35ft^3 in ES.

TECHNICAL: **engine types**: 1780, then 1985cc from 1969, both four-cyl. petrol; **gearbox**: four-speed manual, (rare) automatic and overdrive initially optional; **suspension**: (front) independent coil spring enclosing dampers with anti-roll bars, (rear) rigid axle with transverse Panhard rod and coil springs; **brakes**: disc front and drum rear (models from 1970 had rear disc).

TRIM: Leather.

KEY OPTIONAL EXTRAS: Overdrive (then standardised), Minilite alloy or Dunlop light metal rims (1800E/ES), tinted windows from August 1970, air-conditioning (later cars), fabric sunroof.

Clover Rim alloy wheel from an 1800E.

140 & 160 SERIES

Following the end of production of the PV544 in late 1965, and amongst rumours of a new five-seater car produced at the new factory facility near Gothenburg airport, the new 140 model series cars were filtered in to run alongside the sister Amazon range for four years, soon snapping at the heels of Audi, Triumph, Rover, Vauxhall and various Humbers and Zephyrs. With similar mechanicals and a tough reputation to maintain, the 140 series lasted for eight years and proved very popular with the existing customer base. The new 140 and later 160 series cars were the forerunners to the autumn 1974-launched 200 series, which lasted well into the 1990s, proving this was a reliable, long-lasting platform utilising a variety of engines and body styles throughout production in several international locations.

Initially powered by the 1778cc B18 engine used in the 120 series, the 140 won the Swedish Automobile Association gold medal and diploma for Volvo, for its new Girling dual circuit braking system featuring four-wheel disc brakes, which allowed for 80 per cent capacity braking if one system failed, retaining service to at least one side of the rear axle. Pop-out safety laminated windscreens, energy absorbing front and rear ends, burst-proof door locks, front seats designed to reduce whiplash in an accident, and a special jointed steering column design to snap in the event of a heavy collision added to the list of new safety features. There were 8000 spot welds used on each car's construction, each one strong enough to support the vehicle's entire body weight. Surprisingly, for the right-hand drive markets, the windscreen wipers were never placed on the opposing arc on any 144, 145 or 164, meaning there was always a blind spot for taller drivers in rainy conditions.

The first glimpse of the new Volvo 140 series came mid-August 1966, when Volvo issued two press pictures to the motoring press: a three-quarter front photo depicting the new longer, lower and sleeker lines of a 144 saloon next to a Swedish lake, and a side profile photo looking into the 144's interior with its 'B' post physically removed. Displayed

The first 144 off the production line in 1966.

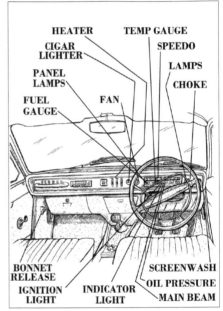

First dashboard designation of the 144/145 series, with earlier long gear lever.

The author in 1980 with his very early B18 144. Great registration looking back!

Although marketed in the UK, the 142 sold much more successfully in continental Europe.

clearly are Volvo's own lap-and-diagonal safety belts that had been fitted by Volvo to all new cars for some time. Volvo launched its 142 two-door saloon and 144 four-door saloon to supplement its ongoing P120s. All early models were built as left-hand drive, with Sweden soon to change its driving habits forever, as it moved over to driving on the right to match most of Europe. New cars were built as left-hookers well in advance in readiness for the overnight change on 3rd September 1967.

UK prices were yet to be set, but it was anticipated the new model would cost a little more than contemporary Amazon cars. The interior was smart and functional, the fully adjustable front seats designed by an orthopaedic surgeon with unique (until the late 1960s VW 411) adjustable lumbar pads with a 'Firm/Soft' knob on the side of the seat. Headrests were still a future feature however ...

Opposite the Porsche stand at the Earl's Court London Motor Show in October 1966, an unregistered white 144 was displayed in the UK for the first time. If registered this early car would have qualified for a 'D' suffix, never seen on a 144 as all press cars adorned the short-lived Suffolk 'E' suffix, 'BJ,' 'DX,' 'PV' and 'RT,' all assigned to the Ipswich (UK Volvo Concessionaires) area. Soon after the

announcement came that two models were initially available: the 75hp single carburettor 144 and the more powerful 100hp 144S.

When prices were announced by the following April, including car taxes the 144 retailed at £1354, and the sportier 144S at £1415, compared to £1065 for the entry level 132S Amazon at the time. Automatic transmission soon became an option for an extra £86 on the 144, and by the end of the year £24 could be saved by opting for the 142 model: a very rare sight on UK roads, the two-door also being offered in faster 'S' form. When selected, engine revs dropped by over 10 per cent to aid long distance economy if the option of overdrive was requested; this was available on the 'S' versions, and a badge was fitted on the left side of the rear panel. By the end of 1966 the factory had produced between 3-4000 of the new cars. In Sweden, Norway and Holland the Volvo 144 was voted 'Car of the Year.'

Following sightings at the factory of a trickle of right-hand drive cars in February 1967, in the very early spring of that year there was a somewhat unusual event in Suffolk. In a variety of colours, dozens of 144s were driven in procession uphill away from Volvo Concessionaires Ltd, south of Ipswich docks, destined for eager dealers across the UK.

All were adorned with windscreen stickers, and initially progressed in one long line up Sandyhill Lane and beyond to the nearest petrol station, as the factory supplied the cars with just one gallon. Sadly whilst the large building still stands (with a faint outline of the Volvo sign), the immediate area is now derelict.

These drivers would have found that the earliest UK speedometers were not calibrated that well, indeed *Autocar* magazine reporting later in 1967 "... the worst calibration of any we can remember ..." recording an error of 8mph even at 30mph: possibly, it stated, due to the Pirelli tyres not being accounted for during testing. The odometer had six digits however, good for up to a million miles ...

Just as the P120 range featured a factory-built five-door estate car platform, this time a vertical tailgate was utilised on the very stylish new 145 estate, announced in January 1968. The "down-to-earth and up-to-town estate" really was a masterpiece in automotive design. Within the same wheelbase and overall length as the saloons, the roof line stayed horizontal along its entire length. The rear passenger side doors were taken from the saloons, creating an attractive kick-up style continuing to the rear-most side windows: the earliest models having two glass pieces split vertically, and the rearmost pivoting to allow better through-flow ventilation. Rear suspension and axle specification was uprated over the saloon (it could carry a half a ton payload), and the well-trimmed boot was cavernous at 70ft^3, featuring a handy hidden stowage area under the flat rear floor. There was so much more room than the 144 saloon, which had a high loading sill (its boot lid was effectively just a flap) allowing 21ft^3 of luggage.

The estate's much needed rear wash/wipe system was still optional at this point, but at least the rear screen was heated. An extra interior light was fitted in the load area, and the rear seating was a single fold-down affair. The rear bumper matched the saloon's, and attractive vertical tail lamp clusters gripped the 'D' pillars, allowing for easy entry for goods under the top hinged tailgate, which would open high enough to assist an average height driver when loading in poor weather conditions. Overall, the 145 estate was 9 per cent more

An early production 145 estate. The initial UK price listing was £1523 in April 1968.

The capacious 71ft^3 interior of a 1972 145 estate, in red. The robust short pile trim proved very hard-wearing.

expensive than the 144 saloon (£1522) for the entry level version, and only slightly heavier. Volvo (UK) also boasted at the time of the estate's launch that the factory had spent £15 million on UK parts to build its cars in Sweden. New cars had no import duty, as Sweden was one of the UK's EFTA partners. Overall, for every two saloons sold, one estate would leave the sales room, which was proportionally much higher than competitor's figures.

Production of the B20 2-litre engine started by August 1968, and it now replaced the smaller engines in cars. The move from 1778cc to 1986cc was achieved by increasing the even more over-square engine bore from 84.1 to 88.9mm. Improvements were made to the valves, which were larger on the inlet side, and the oil pump's capacity was increased by 50 per cent. Further enhancements were made to the viscous coupling (its maximum speed now 3000rpm), and closed-circuit crankcase breathing was standard across the range using the factory-sealed Zenith Duplex system. New full exhaust emission control was a first for a European manufacturer. There was no price rise until later in the year, and model ranges continued unchanged, with a base model and twin carburettor 'S' version still available on 142s, 144s and 145s. Overall, the extra 15hp accelerated the cars from 0-60mph in about the same time; the new engines were designed for improved torque and sheer pulling power rather than out and out performance, with contemporary road testers commenting on the smoothness and quietness of the new motors.

Externally, a B20 motif was fitted to the front grille. Upholstery improvements were also brought in at this point, as was a different range of colours. The 1800 coupé also enjoyed this engine upgrade. Worthing-based Ruddspeed Engineering had by now offered a conversion on the B20-engined cars, with stiffer and lowered suspension, improved acceleration (shaving off at least 2 seconds from the 0-60mph figures), and higher top speed (around 8mph more) through improvements to the cylinder head. In 1969, *Autocar* magazine described the car as "rorty and sporty."

The luxuriously-appointed 164 four-door saloon made its debut at the 55th Paris Salon in early October 1968. Distinctive by way of its Vanden Plas Princess R-inspired large square front grille, with a bandolier-style emblem across its vertical slats, itself a callback to the 1920s Volvos, the 164 was offered with the all-new B30 3-litre six-cylinder engine: its design based on the existing 144 B20 pushrod power unit. This was Volvo's first six-cylinder car since the PV60, which was discontinued in 1950. More engine bay length was needed for an in-line six, so to accommodate this the wheelbase was increased by nearly 4in ahead of the 'A' pillar, but behind the front axle line. A floating headlamp design was utilised,

First production 164. No fog lamps, but with vent covers instead, and the model continued like this in the USA.

This dates to around 1972: a left-hand drive 164 engine bay with 3-litre straight six carburettor engine.

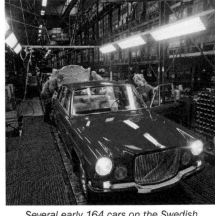

Several early 164 cars on the Swedish production line.

creating an attractively curved bonnet. Further 5in diameter round grilles were employed either side of the radiator, diagonally below the headlamp line, although the Paris show car had the optional front auxiliary lighting instead (non-US specification). New variable ratio steering gear was used, as the car weighed 175lb more than its existing four-cylinder sister vehicles, with the 144's front weight bias of 51 per cent increasing to 55 per cent for the heavier car.

Deeper pile fully fitted carpets, a teak inlay on the full-width vertical dashboard (the

The earliest dash style of the 140/160 series. This is the top-end 164 with later wooden veneer and blue trim.

Cutaway drawing of the early model 164 in the late 1960s. The engine is a straight six 3-litre.

teak was seen on late 1971 144/5 cars), and extra stainless steel trim along the sills, around the wheelarches and lower panel below the boot lid completed the look. A large and distinctive 164 badge was fitted on the left side of the rear panel. Extra sound deadening, sumptuously contoured broad-pleat leather seat upholstery by Connolly, and a fold-down centre armrest on the rear seat were luxury features. On the backs of the front seats were strong storage nets. Remarkably, the 164 lacked a clock.

The new gearbox, with its own set of revised ratios designed for the larger engine, utilised a remote gear lever; the unforgettable long shift of the early 140 series was never fitted. Borg-Warner automatic transmission with a higher drive ratio was an optional extra, as was a steering column stalk-activated overdrive facility (top gear on manual cars only), and a sunroof. Much needed optional power steering brought lock-to-lock turns down from 5 to 3.7, with a remarkable turning circle under 29ft. Fifteen inch wheels replaced the 14in units employed on the 144/5 models. Being no slouch, the larger engine 164 could out-accelerate the 144 in the 0-60mph run by around 1.5 seconds. The extra length was enough for the 164 to be in the same Dover-Calais ferry price category.

No factory estate version of the 164 was ever marketed, although several privately produced conversions within classic car circles are often seen at European shows. A red complete knock-down (CKD) example was reputed to have been built in Australia at the Volvo assembly plant for the Managing Director in early 1972, using new unregistered 164 and 145 cars, and featuring manual overdrive transmission. In Sweden, some long-wheelbase (131½in) conversions were used in airport transfer runs with multiple seating, their additional length evident on both the rear side doors and immediately behind, with the rear side door's trailing edges vertical. Furthermore, a special Zagato-bodied 164, the 3000 GTZ, was built in 1970 and exhibited at the Geneva Motor Show, strictly as a one-off two-door 2+2 coupé, following on from the 2-litre 144-based B20 GTZ in 1969.

Later in 1974, Lex Brooklands of Sheffield, UK, shoe-horned a fuel-injected 164 engine into a late model 145 estate to produce a 120mph car of unique character. A top specification 164 TE was produced right at the end of production in 1974 for the UK, German and Australian markets (see following section), available in metallic Gold, Light Blue and Sea Green.

A lack of face-level cold air ventilation brought about the much needed improvement for the 1970 model year in autumn 1969, with a new through-flow air system adopted in all cars, although press reports still criticised the ventilation into the mid-1970s. The 144 series also had a heated rear screen to match the 145 estate and 164, and, following cessation of imports in August 1969, by the end of the year the 142 was quietly dropped from the UK price lists. Front-seat adjustable headrests were standardised across the range on revised seating. The 145s were now fitted with a rear wash-wipe system as standard – a world first for an estate car. The smoked-glass interior mirror was uprated to a manual dipping one, and hazard warning flashers were fitted across the range. The 164 now had its front fog lamps standardised (although not in all markets), as was tinted glass.

Summer 1970 saw the introduction of a second generation front end for the 144/5 cars: a modern three-piece grille with recessed black slats, a stainless steel border and the diagonal bandolier-style mounted motif, similar to the existing 164 arrangement. The 142 kept the earlier stainless steel one-piece grille (and thinner wheels ...), as did the 145 Express, both losing the B20 grille emblem and making way for the round Volvo badge instead. Giving around 120bhp, Bosch fuel-injection was announced but not immediately available for the Grand Luxe, and the new leather-trimmed 144 GL was tuned for 130bhp. This new top 144 model also featured a steel sliding sunroof; the 145 GL estate would have to wait for another year. The standard 144 and 144S models were replaced by the new De Luxe-badged car at this time.

Wider wheel rims, thicker brake discs, improved corrosion resistance and a greater cooling capacity were also introduced. On the estate, gone were the distinctive split rearmost

1979, and an Essex ford tackled at speed in the author's father's 1972 145E.

car performance. Almost 110mph and 0-60mph in a shade over 10 seconds was achievable. These B20F 145E models used a higher compression engine and strengthened gearbox. The electronic brain for the system sat under the driver's seat (it was easy for a heavier driver to bottom out on this unit!), but the fuel pump was often noted as noisy, giving a constant hum. The new injected 112mph 164E cost £2623 (£187 more than the normally-aspirated 164s). It was a worthy rival to the big Rover 3500 P6, shod with wider, lower profile 185/70 Goodyear Grand Prix tyres and uprated shock absorbers.

At the end of 1971, for the princely sum of £45 the 145 estate could be ordered with a set of rear-facing seats that could easily accommodate two children or smallish adults in the boot area. These were cleverly engineered to fit in the existing extra space found under the rear floor (which remained flat when the seats were not deployed) and could simply be popped up and quickly folded open. Using chrome tubing, this well trimmed bench seat had an armrest on each side and flip up headrests, and proved very popular with growing families. Cars so equipped could be

side windows; improved ventilation saw the introduction of a small black rear air extraction vent at the very back of the (UK offside) rear flank. The 164 saw even wider wheels and improvements to its automatic transmission.

The 145 B20 cars (and soon the 144) could be ordered with early Bosch fuel-injection from late 1971, developing 125bhp at 6000rpm, taking them into near sports

Dating to around 1972, still on early dashboards, a 144 and 145 equipped with new recessed door handles and black three-piece grilles.

identified when the seats were stowed by way of the extra bolt heads visible in the carpet. At around the same time, the traditional door latches on all 144, 145 and 164s gave way to sturdy recessed units that modernised the whole appearance from the side profile, and gave a quieter ride at higher speeds. Other manufacturers slowly copied this trend throughout the 1970s.

A remote gear lever, set further back and now floor-mounted, improved the gear change experience in the 140s (manual 164s already had a remote lever) this change now allowing room for a clock on the revised centre panel behind, replacing the previous simple snap-on fuse cover. The steering wheel was restyled to ease instrumentation viewing, but still seemed too large. A Volvo 144 GT was marketed in the UK by TAD (Tungston Automobile Developments of Finchley, north London) largely made from parts supplied directly from the Swedish factory. It featured an exchange head with machined combustion chambers, revised camshaft, a free-flow exhaust manifold, a pair of Solex 45 DDH carburettors, altered air-box and lightened flywheel. For £210 plus fitting, the acceleration was improved and an extra 5mph was added to top speed over the standard 144. Koni dampers all round stiffened up the ride, and the interior boasted four circular instruments in place of the strip speedometer on earlier conversions. A new steering wheel sported a GT badge in the centre, and adverts were abound in the weekly motoring press.

Although appearing in some UK brochures, the unusual high-roof 145 Express would have been an exceptionally rare sight on UK roads, as it was never officially offered, despite a press release being published in March 1972. This model had some stainless steel trim deleted, and was fitted with tough internal skid rails to protect the rear cargo area. Back seats were not fitted. Additionally, a non-glazed metal panel version was also offered. Both versions adopted a very tall rear tailgate, still quite light in operation.

In 1972, to further endorse the safety aspect, the USA Volvo marketeers ran an advertisement asking "Are you in the market for a hardtop?" whereby seven 144 saloons

The high roof 145 Express commercial sold on the continent; this model circa 1972. It retained the earlier front grille arrangement and lack of chrome around the rear side window.

The 145 Express was often used as a school taxi in rural Sweden. Front section roof racks were standard fitting.

were stacked over 30ft (9m) vertically to boast the car's durability – by now 10,000 spot welds at manufacture made the monocoque for increased body strength. Flood damaged vehicles from the docks (these had been destined for scrap) were utilised in this novel stunt; it proved effective, and the idea was later used in other markets with other Volvo models.

By now, Volvo car sales were up by nearly 50 per cent in the UK, and late summer 1972 saw the introduction of many important modifications across the 140 and 160 range. Most noticeable was the entire redesign of the front end which gave rise to a wider, lower look. The front and (saloon) rear indicator units were enlarged and the 144 GL and 164s were fitted with more powerful H4 headlamps. The 144/5s had a much refreshed plastic grille, and the 164's grille height was reduced.

Anodized aluminium front and rear bumpers also had a refresh across the range, with a more attractive ribbed look to the rubber mouldings. The 164 retained its front bumper-mounted indicator and side lamps, but by now the bumper was a fully horizontal unit, replacing the earlier cow-horn design, with no downward curvature under the grille. Even the badging of the range received a makeover, with the manufacturer's name no longer used on the front wings, just the model number. A small, almost unnoticed change was the adoption of a small chrome finishing piece added to the top of each 'C' post on the 144 and 164 saloons, painted black on some later models such as the 142 GT.

A later 164 with fog lamps and second generation bumpers.

Whilst the earlier seats remained, the rest of the interior received a full makeover. The inaccurate strip speedometer was replaced by several modern dials within an entirely new dashboard, featuring (at last!) four air vents, two purely for cold air only. However, *Autosport* magazine's March 1973 road tester still commented: "In Sweden, hot breathing air may be acceptable, but here it is useless. If the heater is operating, the breathing air suffocates the occupants, the alternative being frozen feet!" – the only major fault reported by its tester on 164E YPV163L. In true 1970s fashion interior trim was often a bright colour, such as orange seating and carpets.

A handy glove-box was fitted to the passenger side within the new dash. The 144 GL and 164 cars were also fitted with a rev counter. The heater (itself revised) now had horizontal ventilation switches that were redesigned and moved to a new stylish centre console at its base, and rear ventilation vents were visible under the rear screen on the saloon. There was now room for a radio cassette unit. The windscreen wiper switchgear was no longer knob-operated, but now by way of a three-position steering column stalk. The oversize steering wheel diameter was finally reduced by 1½in, its large padded centre boss protecting a driver in the event of a serious accident. New impact protection was fitted inside the doors, and the rear doors had child-proof safety catches as standard. Overall steering modifications meant it was lighter, at 4.4 turns lock-to-lock. The only modifications in the engine area were revisions to the mounts.

If the motoring public could not get to the October 1973 London Motor Show, with 185 Volvo dealers across the UK, there was plenty of opportunity to inspect the final

The extra length needed for the straight six engine of the 164 is evident here on the longer front wing.

With 'B' post removed for a better view, this 1973 144 GL with bright red interior was one of the last models made with front quarterlights.

A 1973 model year 164 interior. Radios were always optional extras; this one survives as standard without one. The 164E's final new car price in the UK was £3387 (manual) and £3476 (automatic) as late as January 1975.

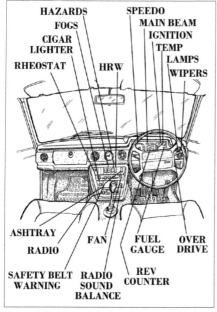

Second dashboard designation, from 1973-74 season cars.

incarnation of the 140 and 160 series from late 1973; indeed, until the summer/autumn 1974 introduction of the 200 series. Included on the motor show stand was an impressive 144 cutaway car, plus the refreshed models in newly available colours. To the casual eye, the most obvious change was the US-inspired energy absorbing bumpers, which paved the way to the new Federal-ready 200 series soon to be announced. Noticeable at the front was

a gap between bumper and body, while at the rear a rubber insert was present to prevent road grime being sucked up. These bumpers took the cars into a new cross channel ferry price band, being over 15ft 6in long.

The earlier screw off small petrol cap on the offside back of the rear flank was replaced by a larger front-hinged fuel flap lower down on the same side, following the relocation of the fuel tank to just behind the rear axle. Its capacity increased in size slightly from 12¾ gallons (58 litres) to 13¼ gallons (60 litres). As a result, the saloon's boot was a little bigger. Inside a new warning lamp illuminated when a driving lamp had failed and passengers failing to belt up caused another lamp to come on. Front seat heaters were now fitted to the leather clad 144 GL and 164, activating below 14°C (57°F), and the seat base design was improved for added safety. A flame-resistant material was used in the cloth versions. The better K-Jetronic fuel-injection replaced the earlier Bosch electronic version, although 144E power was down from 124 to 115bhp, but at least two-star petrol could be used. The fuel pump was revised and insulated, and proved less noisy. The B20 engine's compression ratio was reduced from 10.2 to 8.7:1 on such models. A smart brushed aluminium 'Fuel-injection' badge was fitted to the rear panel on the right. Finally, the quarterlight windows on the front doors were deleted, allowing the frames to be welded to the doors for better

The last incarnation of the 144: a 1974 metallic gold GL with big thick rubber-faced bumpers.

Large format bumpers seen again on this last generation 145 estate. Headlamp washers and by now quarterlight windows had been deleted.

roll-over protection, giving a cleaner, more modern appearance, reducing wind noise, and affording extra visibility.

Following the recent demise of the carburettor 164, the six-cylinder range was increased with a new 'limited numbers available' executive that must be the holy grail of the 140/160 range: the 164 TE, which cost a whopping extra £570 on the UK market over a standard 164E. A UK press advertisement displaying a TE with rear headrests read: "It's sophisticated fittings include: air-conditioning

throughout; eight-track stereo and radio with four speakers; electrically operated aerial; tinted glass; sunroof; adjustable rear reading lights; headlamp washers and wipers; power steering and a fully carpeted boot." Hailed as a limousine (it retained the standard wheelbase, however), it seemed expensive at just over £4000. An example was also on display at the 1973 London Motor Show. Unusually, the TE badges were left in the glovebox for dealer fitting.

Recessed door handles, 164 wheel with chrome ring, chrome petrol cap with Volvo insignia, last generation 140 series indicators, 164 front indicators, and 1973 season rear lamps.

A selection of 140/160 series badges through the years.

For several years after the 140 series had ceased production, *Autocar* magazine kept hold of its trusty March 1973-registered metallic blue 145E RGT220L until it had covered 112,000 busy miles, often towing exhibition trailers and moving large amounts of publishing material around, fitted with a full length Armadillo boot liner option and roof rack. At the time it was the magazine's longest running test car, before finally being sold in 1978 after nearly six years of continual use. Listed below are the type of issues that occurred during *Autocar*'s lengthy liaison with the vehicle, which it documented so well in various articles during that period. Excluding routine servicing and tyres, brake pads, belts and bulbs, the following extra works were performed:

12,000 miles: replacement tailgate lock barrel and bonnet release cable.

18,000 miles: new clutch driven plate and cover, thrust bearing, tailgate strut renewed.

20,000 miles: new water pump.

45,000 miles: exhaust received attention as did rust on door jams.

49,000 miles: new exhaust fitted.

56,000 miles: new heater motor.

63,000 miles: leaking core plug issues.

65,000 miles: broken clutch cable replaced.

68,000 miles: another new bonnet cable fitted.

70,000 miles: another broken clutch cable replaced.

72,000 miles: another broken tailgate lock replaced.

73,000 miles: rust on doors and sills corrected.

74,000 miles: new clutch plate, cover and bearing.

75,000 miles: repairs to the tailgate lock again.

82,000 miles: new exhaust, gearbox mount, steering idler bush, wash/wipe switch replaced, new oil pressure switch, resetting of fuel-injection system, new fuel hoses, LT and chassis earthing leads.

At 84,200 miles: new speedo head and inlet manifold.

At 88,000 miles: new water pump and viscous coupling, rebuilt propshaft, new bonnet cable catch.

At 106,000 miles: new tailgate strut again.

At 110,000 miles: replacement engine mounts.

Note: Bar's Leaks was poured into the engine a year before sale, and was holding up well after a cracked cylinder head had been detected. Overall 115 pints of oil were used, and average fuel consumption was around 23mpg, meaning the car had actually consumed its own weight in petrol ...

From the list, we can see the 145 had a hunger for tailgate locks and struts, clutch parts and various cables! Back in the day, the author always wondered what had become of the car after spotting it locally, and in this digital age we can have a look ... According to the UK DVLA website, RGT220L was taxed only until summer 1984 and has not been on the road since – sadly we assume scrapped, falling well short of the average Volvo 14-year lifespan. It is only fair to point out that the car had received a very hard life, by the magazine staff's own admission, including heavy towing, like so many 145s often spotted well-laden with heavily overloaded trailers at agricultural auction houses, or towing horse-boxes at equestrian events etc. This car last changed hands in January 1980.

Following the announcement of the new 200 series in August 1974, the 140 series were listed in the new price tables until October 1974, ranging between £2155 (144 DL) and £3014 (145E DL automatic) mirroring the time when the new 200 series models were on display at the London Motor Show. The 164E and 164 TE were available in the UK for a short while after, sharing the price lists with the new 244 and 245 cars, just creeping into January 1975. The final retail price in the weekly motoring press listings was the 164E at £3387 (manual), £3476 (automatic) and top-end 164 TE leaving the list earlier in October 1974 at £3946. There was no noticeable price increase for the new 200 series cars.

140/164 series media advertising slogans
Created in Sweden with all the care in the world (144, 1967)
Who wants a car with engineered ashtrays? (144, 1967)
Who cares about rubber-cushioned bumpers? (144, 1967)
The down-to-earth and up-to-date estate car (145, 1968)
A most rewarding part of owning a Volvo is selling it (144, 1968)
Volvo buy British – buy Volvo (144, 1968)
What does reliability mean to you? (144, 1968)
Discover 2-litre power when you open up (144, 1969)

Buy a car that won't self-destruct in three years (144 USA, 1969)
Poor man's Rolls-Royce? Actually a rich man's Volvo (164 USA, 1969)
Get out from car payments ... elegantly (164 USA, 1969)
If the brakes ever failed, nobody would ever notice (144, 1969)
Now a 3-litre for the lively minded (164, 1969)
Fat cars die young! (144, USA 1970)
Cars shouldn't just be built for showroom traffic (144 USA, 1970)
The fuel-injected Volvo 142E. Open her up and you're in for some surprises (1971, USA)
Volvos come in blue, green, white, yellow and red. No rust (144 USA, 1971)
True economy isn't miles to the gallon, it's more years to the car (144 USA, 1971)
The GT eater (144, 1972)
The earth shall inherit the weak (144 USA, 1972)
Why safety sells in Sweden (144 USA, 1972)
The kind of car everyone's trying to build (144 USA, 1972)
In a nation of engineers, bad cars don't sell (144 USA, 1972)
In Sweden you drive a good car or else (144 USA, 1972)
Inside every Volvo comes this big comfortable car (144 USA, 1972)
A car shouldn't have disc brakes just to make it sell better (144 USA, 1973)
In most countries, the best selling car is also cheap. Not in Sweden (144 USA 1972)
Are you in the market for a hardtop? (7 144s stacked up, USA 1972)
The power and the glory for ever and ever (164 Australia, 1972)
Hard to keep your mind on the road when your back is killing you (144, 1973 USA)
Volvo's most vital statistic: 60 to 0 in under 4 seconds (144 Australia, 1973)
Motoring for extra performance (TAD 144 GT, 1973)
It could embarrass most sports cars (Rudd 144, 1973)
What makes the Volvo 145 the most wanted big estate (145, 1973)
Why people who can afford any of this year's luxury cars will buy the Volvo (164, 1973)
The rich need Volvos too (164 USA, 1973)

A civilised car built for an uncivilised world (164 USA, 1973)

True luxury is more car to the foot. Not more feet to the car (USA 164, 1973)

Your kind of luxury in Volvo's kind of car (164E)

Why don't all cars carry a 12 month unlimited mileage guarantee? (144, 1973)

It shines where the other new cars shine. And where they don't (144, 1973)

Volvo's owner protection plan (smashed 142)

There's a new Volvo waiting for you at your local (144/5, 164, 1973)

The Volvo 164 TE: a limited edition (164 TE, 1973)

Luxury is built in. Not tacked on (1974 USA 164)

Choosing a Volvo has certain built-in advantages (144, 1974)

Really, it's a bit of a wolf in sheep's clothing (144E, 1974)

How long will it take for all of Volvo's safety features to become law? (144, 1974)

It eats up the miles without drinking up the petrol (144E, 1974)

True luxury is more car to the foot. Not more feet to the car (164 USA, 1974)

Luxury is built in. Not tacked on (164 USA, 1974)

A civilised car built for an uncivilised world (164 USA, 1974)

Your kind of luxury in Volvo's kind of car (164 Australia, 1974)

Driving a luxury car doesn't mean you have money to burn (164 Australia, 1974)

140/160 BODY TYPES: two-door and four-door saloons, five-door estate; **manufactured at:** Torslanda (Sweden), Ghent (Belgium), Halifax (Canada), Melbourne (Australia), Shah Alam (Malaysia) and Durban (South Africa);

number produced: 1,360,179 (all 140/160 types) – 412,986 (142), 523,808 (144), 268,317 (145), 155,068 (164); **production span:** 142 and 144 saloons, 1966-1974, 164 four-door saloon, 1968-1974, 145 five-door estate, 1967-1974, 145 enclosed and glazed van (Express), 1968-1974.

PERFORMANCE: top speed: 100mph/160kph (144), 120mph/195kph (164E); **0-60mph/100kph:** 12 sec (144), 10 sec (164E); **average economy:** 22-27mpg (144/5), 18-23mpg (164).

PRICE AT LAUNCH: £1354 (144), £1523 (145), £1791 (164).

MEASUREMENTS: length: (add 5in for larger 1974 rubber bumper models) 15ft 3in (4.64m) (144/5), 15ft 6in (4.72m) (164); **width:** 5ft 8in (1.73m); **height:** 4ft 8in (1.44m), **wheelbase:** 8ft 10½in (2.7m) (144/5), 8ft 6½in (2.65m) (164); **weight:** 2696lb (1224kg) (144), 2822lb (1281kg) (145), 3192lb (1450kg) (164); **wheels:** 15in; **turning circle:** 28ft 6in (8.69m); **fuel capacity:** 12.8 gallons/58 litres (1966-73), 13¼ gallons/60 litres (1973-74); **boot capacity:** 21.7ft^3 (saloon), 71ft^3 (estate).

TECHNICAL: engine types: 1778cc 1966-67, then 1986cc 1968-74, both four-cyl petrol on 144/5, 2979cc six-cyl in-line petrol (164); **gearbox:** four-speed manual 1966-74, automatic three-speed and then overdrive fitted on later manual cars; **suspension:** (front) independent wishbones, coil (rear) live axle with coil springs, Panhard rod; **brakes:** disc front and rear.

TRIM: vinyl, cloth and leather.

KEY OPTIONAL EXTRAS: built-in front fog lamps, 3rd row of seats on the 145, tow bar, Armadillo boot liner (in either half or full length sizes) popular on estate models, air-conditioning, automatic transmission, sunroof.

DUTCH 66 & 300 SERIES CARS

Daf had been car building since the late 1950s after the introduction of its belt-driven car at the Amsterdam Motor Show in Holland in February 1958. This was the first production car to offer continuously variable transmission since the UK Clyno of the 1920s. Alas, the Wolverhampton company eventually folded due to financial issues. The system was technically unique, being infinitely variable, and ensuring an ideal engine speed at all times with no transmission jerks, being ultra smooth at all times, although there were criticisms of crunching occurring when getting the car into gear initially.

Over a 17-year period, Daf offered three basic types of belt-driven cars:

Daf 600, 750, Daffodil 30, 31, 32 and 33 series (1958-1967)
Daf 44 (1966-1974), Daf 46 (1974-1976) (Michelotti design)
Daf 55 (1967-1972,) Daf 66 (1972-1975) (Michelotti design)

The earliest cars were saloon only, whilst the 44 was also available as an estate, and the 55 and 66 as coupé versions. From certain angles, the later cars bore a resemblance to the Triumph 1300 and later Dolomite cars as they shared the same Italian designer, Giovanni Michelotti. Michelotti had also reworked some of the design features of the Daf 31 prior to its announcement in 1963.

By September 1972, the six-year-old Daf body design could almost be taken to be a pre-production Volvo 66, or at least as a late styling exercise. Replacing the previous curved nose, by now the Daf had adopted a revised vertical black grille upfront. SL was the entry level model, and the sportier Marathon version had twin inset spotlights. In March 1973, when in Vienna, Volvo director Bengt Darnfors said the firm was considering a future "little DAF-Volvo car," with an eye on the Italian lines of the 66, commenting that the venture was then only at an idea stage, with Volvo having bought one third of Daf shares the year before (a 75 per cent stake was achieved in 1975). In

1974, the Variomatic patents were transferred to VDT (Van Doorne Transmissie), which was acquired by Bosch in 1995.

Volvo 66

After the early September 1975 announcement there was a massive Daf model shake-up. The little Daf 66 cars were quickly rebadged as Volvos the following month, albeit with some mechanical and cosmetic changes, but still retained their lively 1289cc four-cylinder air-cooled Renault 12 engine on top models (and all cars for the UK market). The elderly Daf 44 stopped, whilst the 46 model was still imported to the UK for a few months after the merger announcement but

Two new 66s driven in Europe. The front one is a GL with extra spot lamps.

An early 66 GL estate with solid headrests. The Volvo bumpers fitted when the 66 was rebadged were more in keeping with the Swedish parentage.

*Wooden dashboard finish and reclining seats
for the Volvo 66.*

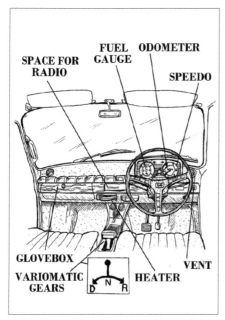

Dashboard designation on the Volvo 66.

stayed badged as Daf, costing just over three-quarters the amount of the Volvo badged 66. In Europe, a 1.1-litre version Volvo 66 was also offered. Like a Porsche 944, the transmission was under the boot floor at the rear, and unlike many new competitors that had by now progressed to a front-wheel drive arrangement, the 66 was still rear wheel driven. By early 1976, Volvo had successfully overturned the elderly-person's image of the previous Daf 66 by appealing to younger drivers, and the order backlog was over 1000 units by spring that year.

The opening UK prices for the Volvo badged cars were £1945 (saloon) and £2095 (for the estate), 20 per cent more expensive than the previous top specification Daf 66 Marathon cars. However, allowing for the model revisions still represented fair value for money.

Initially, the car was available in six colours in the UK (red, brown, white, yellow and aubergine) quickly followed by metallic blue and with two interior trim options (black or light brown). Metallic green, however, appeared on an early UK press car, LGV67P, and the colour was offered later. The new 66 GL continued in the UK and other markets with the attractive Daf Marathon style side and boot striping decals seen earlier, although in production these decals were not fitted to cars with metallic paint. In addition, the Daf 66 Marathon's twin halogen spot lamps were a standard fitment, alongside main beam lighting. The new alloy front wing badges were contemporary Volvo style and featured the familiar castellations at their tops with the engine size depicted in litres under the 66 name. Gone now for good, however, was the attractive fastback Daf coupé derivative. The GL estate model was fitted with a rear wash wipe system as standard after a few months into production, not seen on previous Dafs, although it did look a bit of an afterthought. Laminated screens, an energy absorbing body, rubber-covered impact bumpers front and rear and twin speed wipers were some of the safety features fitted, and the wipers were now black. Integral head restraints were a solid format initially, but soon after production started the 66 had the trademark

Volvo 244-inspired headrests with the see-through horizontal slats. A mechanical change to the transmission brought in a centrifugal clutch that disconnected as soon as the gear lever was touched, thus there were no more crunching noises when forward or reverse were selected, or creeping forward (or back) with the choke out – an annoying built-in affliction for the previous Dafs. Other modifications were enhanced noise insulation, a redesigned centre console and improved corrosion resistance.

Volvo distributor Brooklands Motors of Birmingham arranged a trial run for its dealers in hilly areas of Cherbourg, northern France in early October 1975. *Autocar* magazine tagged along too, hoping one day to do its own full road test, but this was never to happen. It commented: "At 75mph, roadholding was more than adequate and one went through fast bends quite securely (three up) without losing speed, with the car apparently leaning on the outside back wheel."

In fact, most of the UK mainstream motoring press did not road-test the new belt-drive Volvos, as they proved so hard to get hold of from the Ipswich concessionaires. However, some carefully selected local newspapers did managed to get a vehicle; in its 7th November 1975 issue, the *Surrey Mirror* tester Kimble Earl stated of the 66 GL estate model, registered KPJ1P: "The only verdict on the new Volvo 66 is that it's an exceptional car. Distinctive lines, smart finish and good performance combine to produce a memorable motoring experience which I have rarely found equalled." He then went on to compare the Volvo 66's favourable handling to the much missed Mini Cooper.

What Car? was the only major UK magazine to test the 66, in estate form in a group test against a Mk1 VW Golf and Opel Kadett, although the smaller print run *Car Mechanics* tested the estate on its own in August 1976. "It's a pity Volvo didn't modify the switchgear more than they have ... However, haphazardly scattered switches on the dash control the rear screen heater, hazard flashers, lights, rear screen wiper, low gear hold and auxiliary spot lamps – a real mess with no planning at all ..."

The interior was partially updated, although still featuring the existing Daf full solid front headrests integral with the seats (although in wrong place for some drivers), but the illuminated gear indicator was permanently set for continental left-hand drive drivers. This in itself was a major revision over the Daf 66 lever, Volvo adopting the more conventional P-R-N-D setup instead of forward to go forwards, back to go backwards. The gear lever was more sophisticated than the Daf's, and overall the interior had better trim and a heavier look, but with a softer steering wheel. Rear seatbelts were fitted, and inertia reel was standard all round. Access to the rear compartment was made easier by front seats that leaned inwards at the same time as tilting forwards. So well-equipped the Volvo 66 was, it topped the *What Car?* magazine's £1800 to £2400 Value Index Table in a 1977 issue, gaining 15 extra points for having automatic transmission as standard. Journalists pointed out the high engine tone that stayed at one pitch when accelerating until the desired speed was reached, and when braking the revs would again rise to give some degree of engine braking.

Production continued largely unchanged for three years, with some cosmetic changes made for the 1978 model year: the door mirrors went black, and the small round side repeater indicators on the front wings were replaced with larger rectangular units. Sales were now in decline following fiercer competition to the 66's ageing lines, and in October 1978 the model was finally deleted from the UK new car price lists. Final pricing structure was £2757 (saloon) and £2890 (estate), and there was a trickle of 'T' registered examples. At time of writing (April 2023) there are around 36 known survivors with the UK DVLA, out of around 14,000 imported.

In all, around 106,137 Volvo 66 cars were built in the Born factory, Netherlands, selling mainly in Europe until 1980. Estates accounted for 27 per cent of sales, despite this model stopping production earlier in 1978. In Sweden the vehicle seemingly was never accepted as a proper Volvo, and sold poorly, despite sales campaigns. Whilst the UK enjoyed only the top model GL, lesser

A 66 saloon on airport duties, circa 1979. No Daf Marathon style side stripes on this base model.

Later model 66s with see through headrests and smaller wing badging.

specification L and DL versions were marketed in Europe, identified by their single headlamps and lack of stripes. A solitary metallic blue saloon exists in the Daf museum in Eindhoven, Holland, and three are known to have been privately exported to the USA. Given the scarcity of this model now, it is entirely probable that there are more scale models left than the real thing; oddly some of these in non-standard colours!

Away from UK markets, the side badging was updated by 1980; the castellation-style wing badge was replaced with a simple Volvo insignia on each side. During that year, a dealer gave disabled drivers in the Shetland Islands in Scotland the use of twenty-three 66 and 343 cars, via a charitable trust fund set up by the oil companies. The Volvos gave better traction, had particularly good seats, automatic transmission and good wheelchair access, and use of the ageing invalid tricycle was stopped, particularly dangerous on the windswept islands in the winter.

66 media advertising titles
The car that has everything – except a gearbox (Daf, 1964)
Daf is only for special families (33 and 44)
The intelligent way to get round these days (1975 Daf 66)
Everything Volvo stands for. Apart from big (dealer sales postcard)
Robust, sporty performance with rugged Volvo reliability (brochure)
Generous inside comfort (brochure)
Crafted in the Volvo tradition (brochure)
The start of something small (brochure)
More space and the extra convenience of a third door (brochure: estate)
The start of something small (pin badge and foldout brochure)
We can think of only two reasons not to buy a big Volvo (66 and 343)

VOLVO 66 BODY TYPES: three-door saloon and estate; **manufactured at**: Born (Netherlands); **number produced**: 106,137; **production span**: 1975-1980.
PERFORMANCE: top speed: 85mph/135kph; **0-60mph/100kph**: 19 sec; **average economy**: 33mpg.

PRICE AT LAUNCH: £1945 (saloon), £2045 (estate).
MEASUREMENTS: length: 12ft 9½in (3.905m); **width**: 5ft 0in (1.525m); **height**: 4ft 8½in (1.44m); **wheelbase**: 7ft 5in (2.26m); **weight**: 1907lb (867kg); **wheels**: 13in; **turning circle**: 31ft 7in (9.63m); **fuel capacity**: 9¼ gallons/42 litres; **boot capacity**: 7.2ft³ (saloon).
TECHNICAL: engine types: 1289cc 1966-67, four-cyl petrol, 1108cc (non UK); **gearbox**: Variomatic CVT automatic only; **suspension**: (front) independent by longitudinal torsion bars, (rear) De Dion axle with single-leaf semi elliptic; **brakes**: front disc, rear drum.
TRIM: Cloth with integral headrests in front.
KEY OPTIONAL EXTRAS: Fog lights, rubber mats, GT road wheels, locking petrol cap, dog guard, rear fog lamps, door pocket, roof rack.

Volvo 300 series

Scrolling back to the early 1970s Dutch scene, Daf had been spending a great deal of effort designing a small to medium sized new model that would still utilise its unique Variomatic transmission. The model was known as P900, planned to become Daf 77 which at the time was the next logical number to use in sequence.

Just a few months after the introduction of the new 66 – and unlike its smaller cousin – it was announced that the 1397cc Renault engine was to be fitted. Volvo adopted its 343 name using the existing Volvo numbering theme, i.e., 300 series, four-cylinder, three-door. Later models would be 345 (five-door), then in the 1980s, simply 340 followed by the bigger engine 360 to bring the range in-line with the larger cars from Sweden; the longer booted saloon version arrived in autumn 1983.

There were two notch-back bodyshells utilised, the three-door and five-door, but no convertibles or estates, although design studies of these formats were carried out. This was the first Volvo hatchback since the P1800. Early left-hand drive, pre-production, hand-built cars made their debut as early as March 1976 at the Geneva Motor Show, where two complete 343s were on the Volvo stand,

An very early production 343 from 1976. Note lack of side rubbing trim, chrome door mirrors/ handle trim and solid headrests. Very few early 343s like this survive. All were Variomatic, as denoted by the air vents seen in the front bumper.

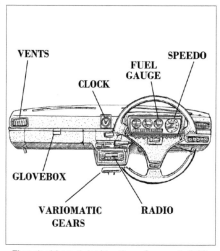

First dashboard designation of an early 343.

with a third car semi-sectioned to show the installation of the Variomatic transmission. Engineers on the stand dismissed the possibility of the model getting standard transmission in the future, although there was a legal struggle to determine whether the Transmatic was included in the original takeover deal.

It would be around six months until the UK saw any right-hand drive imports arrive, although only 727 343s were registered in the UK that first year, not helped by the fact a test car had been spectacularly rolled in a

Goodwood track demonstration – hardly what the Volvo PR guys wanted at the time. In 1977, sales picked up with 2318 sold in the UK, and by 1980 it was 16,718. Over a 15-year production run, all cars were offered on the same 2.4m wheelbase in a variety of guises and running gear, at least until 1983 when a saloon was offered with larger boot space (with four-door shell only). Changes were made by early February 1978, with the CVT belt-drive kickdown operation improved for engine speeds below 1700rpm, and modifications were made to the suspension to reduce body roll. Interiors were improved with restyled seats and trim, and two extra vents were added to improve ventilation.

The 343 started with Variomatic transmission only, but Volvo soon offered the M45 200 series manual gearbox fitted at the rear from late 1978, as it transpired that Europeans were not overly keen on small automatics. The achieve this, the manual 'box was turned on its side and fitted with a modified selector shaft – the gearbox ratios remained unaltered. This action was justified by a large uplift in sales; in the UK registrations were as follows: 2318 in 1977, 4163 in 1978, 10,875 in 1979 and 16,718 in 1980. Performance was improved, too; it proved much quicker in terms of acceleration and top speeds (0-80mph acceleration was ten seconds quicker), and a 7mph top speed improvement was gained (*Autocar* magazine test figures from 1977/78), although performance was still not competitive. However, despite weighing in at nearly one ton at the kerbside, economy was slightly improved, and the manual 343 became a strong rival to the Austin Maxi, Chrysler Horizon, VW Golf and Escort Mk2 estate. Changes also occurring in October 1978 included revised side and rear badging, blackened door mirrors and handles replacing chrome units, a Daf-inspired early Smiths instruments dashboard, which had a comprehensive makeover with new instrument panel and steering wheel, plus heated front seats fitted with 240-style headrests replacing the solid Daf ones. Rear seat passengers now also had their own heating, and rear seat safety belts were standard equipment. On the outside, the front number plate was

By 1978 the 343 had undergone a makeover in the interior. It still had the earlier shorter bumpers, but now sported body side mouldings. This is the DL version with standard wheels; still with the nose cone.

repositioned on the bumper, and side bump strips were evident, as well as new side turn indicators on the wings. The steel wheels had a new appearance, too.

In 1979, the Italian stylist Marcello Gandini of Bertone produced the rather angular Volvo Tundra based on the 343, but this was rejected by Sweden, and the design concept was offered to Citroën. The car was displayed at the 1979 Geneva Motor Show. The four-door 345 model arrived in late 1979, a clever redesign of the rear 'C' pillar made the car look much more integrated, the horizontal base line of the glazed area was extended, with a flick back on the bottom edge of the trailing edge of the rear doors and re-siting of the ventilation. All four quarterlights were fixed. An extra 60lb in weight was added with a slight loss of performance, as to be expected, and the UK received its first imports in January 1980. An early alternative dual-fuel Landi-Hartog LPG option was added an optional extra for cheaper running costs (albeit at a cost to performance which dropped by 20 per cent), at this point extremely popular in the Netherlands. Wheel tracking was also widened at this time.

The option of a GL model was added in September 1980, identified by a front spoiler, tinted glass, rear seat armrest, metallic paint and low profile 175/70SR13 tyres. All models received revised suspension and a higher output fan following earlier criticism, The bumpers were now extended around the body sides and headlamp wash wipes were fitted to

the GL models. The 340 series was now well-established in the top ten cars sold.

Celebrating a 75 per cent increase in UK sales that year, the summer 1981 improvements saw a restyled front end (goodbye to the nose cone!) with integrated front spoiler, bigger rectangular headlamp units with increased intensity (all models had headlamp wash/wipe by now), shallower grille and cleaner bonnet line. The revised bumper had a very slight pointed appearance. Inside the seating was improved with revised shape and trim, and the Volvo media advertising was stepped up, with most of the magazine adverts appearing from this point on, and reference to competitive retail pricing was much evident.

The 343/345 names were changed to 340 and a new 360 arrived autumn 1982, and further improvements were made to the interior, with another new fascia. The top luxury model was now the 360 GLS, and the larger engine models had a bigger fuel tank fitted. Revisions were made to the positioning of the pedals and steering column to give the driver more room and enhanced comfort.

The 360 GLT performance model made its debut in late 1982 following the UK press launch at Longleat House, the Somerset home of the Marquis of Bath. This smart B19A 2-litre model quickly accounted for around 40 per cent of 340/360 sales. The GLT utilised the Bosche LE-Jetronic injection system to rival the Golf GTi and could reach a claimed 112mph, had lowered suspension, heavy-duty dampers and 60 section low profile tyres. Styling upgrades were front air dam, black grille, alloy wheels, rear spoiler and integral fog lamps, whilst a five-speed manual gearbox was standard. The interior was trimmed out in black – including the sombre looking headlining!

In 1982, a van version of the 345 was made available (not for the UK), whereas the rear doors were not glazed, and unlike other European manufacturers it was not based on a three-door shell, but a five-door. The back seat was also removed and uprated suspension was fitted.

Quarterlight windows on the doors were deleted from September 1983 on both two and four-door versions of the 340 and 360, and a five-speed gearbox was standard fitment on the 340 GL. Following extensive European market research performed by Volvo, it was noted that 55 per cent of customers wanted a booted saloon, rather than a hatchback, thus the longer booted 360 GLE joined the range in the UK. Ford had added its Orion (a booted Escort) and Vauxhall offered the Belmont (a saloon based on its Astra), while the four-door only 360 GLE was 4½in longer than the hatchback versions, and the roof had a different pressing due to the revised rear window. These revised models were unveiled at the Frankfurt Motor Show in Germany, with further four-door saloons seen on the continent including the 340. The GLE had alloy wheels, central door locking, electric front windows, headlamp wash/wipe, twin door mirrors and rear seatbelts. It was available in both fuel-injection (115hp) and normally-aspirated (92hp) forms.

The gear ratios were increased by 21 per cent from 1984 with the adoption of the MT5 gearbox. On the continent, 340 cars were offered with 1.6-litre diesel power, but this option never made it to the UK. In late 1985, a quieter 1.7-litre B17 engine became available in addition to the previous smaller units on the 340, and a top specification 340 GLE was available with plenty of extra equipment. A major face-lift occurred at this time: tail lamps were redesigned, wrap-round bumpers with (front) indicators were fitted (these were no longer fitted on the wings), and internally the stylish VDO instruments replaced the original Smiths type. For the UK, the wipers now parked on the 'correct' side for the UK market. Sales continued to rise, resulting in 1986/87

financial year yielding 115,201 units built in the Netherlands, the most ever sold in any 12-month period. In that same year, 26 per cent (30,141) of these were booted four-door 340/360 saloons. In March 1987, a limited edition 340 SE arrived.

Sales of the original Daf Variomatic CVT transmission were down to just a couple of hundred per year on the 1.4-litre 340 cars, which were not avidly marketed. By 1987, a collaboration was made between Van Doorne of Holland, Ford and Fiat, who utilised the CVT in the 1.1-litre Fiesta, Uno and Selecta. Later Mini, Nissan, Audi, Honda and Subaru used this unit, with its manufacture in Tilberg. This later version of the gearbox was a redesign using 300 layered bands of steel, working in compression with each other, rather than tension, and it later saw its way into the 440.

A 340 GLE 'Millionaire' limited edition in 1988 to celebrate a remarkable one million 300 series cars sold overall. This near production run-out model had air-conditioning, electric windows and leather seats. The actual millionth car was finished in red inside and out, and placed in the Dutch Daf museum. The £10,215 340 'Limited Edition' GLE SE (Volvo 60th anniversary) manual model was restricted to 300 units from March 1987, either in Ocean Blue, Light Green, Smoked Silver or Graphite metallic coloured paint with black leather seats, power windows and mirrors plus a sunroof. A 360 version also followed. The 'Red Line' limited edition hatchback was another example in January 1988, suitably adorned with red pinstripes all round, alloy wheels, boot spoiler and uprated appointments. Power-

Volvo Enthusiasts' Club National Rally in 2022. A trio of late 1980s 300 series.

The 340/360 bonnets were always front-hinged. These later models lost the original nose cone.

The 340 could tow 1000kg (braked), although it was unusual to see one with a tow bar.

A 'Red Line' limited edition 340 with hatchback boot open.

The longer four-door 360 gained the extra space in the bigger boot, and rivalled the Ford Orion, Vauxhall Belmont and VW Jetta.

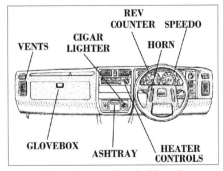

Second generation dashboard.

49

A very tidy 1986 340 DL. The manual gearbox cars had blanking panels over the bumper vent holes, used to cool the Variomatic transmission.

The dashboard of the same 1986 car, a manual low-mileage example in 2022.

Mid-1980s 340 DL. Rear lamp cluster, standard wheels, headlamp wash/wipe and black door handles.

Mid 1980s engine bay for the 340. Note the spare wheel fitment, which freed up space in the boot.

On the three-door models, access was made easier by the provision of these special tipping seat backs.

The 1988 340 Red Line special edition had eye-catching side graphics and red pinstripes all round, including on the bumpers.

The 1987 1.7-litre 360 Limited Edition had a special black leather interior, and was often finished in graphite metallic.

assisted steering became optional equipment in the late 1980s.

The last times the 300 series of cars were listed in the UK market price lists was September 1989 (already alongside the new 440/460 range): for the 2-litre 360 (£10,750-£11,650) and October 1991 for the 1.4- and 1.7-litre 340 five-door hatch, then priced at £9190-£10,100. The 300 series seemingly became more popular which each subsequent revision and overall, 1,086,365 were produced (overall 16 per cent of these were 360s) and

The 360 GLE Limited Edition. Note the boot spoiler.

340/360 media advertising titles
If you want to know what makes a car, ask a man who breaks a car
£6975 won't dent your pocket
Fuel-injection – 115bhp – 5 speed gearbox – 112mph – fog lamps ... (GLT)
It goes lie a BMW. It corners like a Porsche. It stops like a Volvo (GLT)
For anyone who thought they'd never be interested in a Volvo (360 GLT Australia)
Now unleashed, the most sporting Volvo (360 GLT)
When it rains, it shines (360 GLT)
The long short story of the Volvo 343 (foldout brochure)
Bodyguards cost less than Escorts
We wanted to drop by to show you how much less our Volvo cost than your Escort
Protection without Extortion
It hit the ground at 30mph and the dummy who drove it walked away (340)
If you can't see what's new about the Volvo 340, here's an aerial view
The things that work the best don't always cost the most
Volvos start at £4892 (and minus 30 degrees C)
£5270 won't hurt you
Volvo always protect your investment, even if it's only £5166
The paintwork doesn't reflect the price
£5394 isn't a lot of damage
A Ford. Affordable
The steel. The steal
Are you special enough to own a Volvo special edition?
Even at £6890 you won't run in to many
The paintwork doesn't reflect the price

was accidentally placed between Park and Reverse gears. The AA had soon conducted a customer survey and it was alleged that 300 runaway incidents had happened. An independent action group was formed and by 1986, Volvo wrote to 33,000 owners of all cars specifically fitted with Variomatic transmission and supplied a booklet with the correct operating procedure. An 'engineering modification' to the gear selector was fitted after a recall which included an audio and visual warning that reverse had been selected.

300 SERIES BODY TYPES: three-door hatch, five-door hatch, four-door saloon; **manufactured at**: Born (Netherlands), Gothenburg (Sweden), Malaysia and Indonesia (CKD kits); **number produced**: 910,342 (343/5 and 340), plus 176,023 (360), total 1,086,365; **production span**: 1976-1991. **PERFORMANCE: top speed**: 87mph/140kph (early 343), 108mph/175kph (360 GLT); **0-60mph/100kph**: 17 sec (343), 10.5 sec (360 GLT); **average economy**: 25-28mpg. **PRICE AT LAUNCH**: £3455 (1976 343), £6548 (1982 360 GLT). **MEASUREMENTS: length**: hatch, 13ft 9in (4.12m), booted: 14ft 1in (4.3m); **width**: 5ft 5½in (1.66m); **height**: 4ft 6¾in (1.39m); **wheelbase**: 7ft 10¼in (2.4m); **weight**: 2114-2206lb (959-1001kg); **wheels**: 13in; **turning circle**: 29ft 6in (9m); **fuel capacity**: 10 gallons/45 litres (340), 12.5 gallons/57 litres (360); **boot capacity**: 12.8ft^3 (saloon), 9.4ft^3 (hatch). **TECHNICAL: engine types**: 1289, 1397, 1721 and 1986cc, all four-cyl petrol, 1596cc four-cyl diesel (non UK); **gearbox**: five-speed manual, CVT Variomatic on some 340 only; **suspension**: independent coil (front), De Dion semi-elliptic leaf spring (rear); **brakes**: front disc and rear drum. **TRIM**: Cloth, velour, leather. **KEY OPTIONAL EXTRAS**: alloy wheels, radio cassette, extending towing mirrors, tow bar, additional instruments, roof rack.

the model is fondly remembered by some as 'the lemon that came good'.

In the early 1980s, the 340 had some unwelcome publicity resulting in two cars inadvertently moving off in reverse when the ignition engine was started and the gear level

240 & 260 SERIES

Volvo launched the 200 series in August 1974, a direct replacement to the eight year old 140/160 series, although there was some overlap of sales with the earlier cars. There were two distinct model ranges; the 244/5 and 264 cars (an estate 265 followed later) but unlike its predecessor, the 200 series were all based on the same wheelbase which brought production costs down. Furthermore, later into production some 240/260 body parts were also common to each other.

Safety was most evident in this new model, more so than any Volvo in the past. It took its styling cues and many safety features from the VESV, a safety concept car that had been styled in the late 1960s and made public in early 1972 after ten examples had been built. No body panels were carried across (the familiar 140/160 lines were still utilised), but the striking large format bumpers seen on the 200 series certainly bore a resemblance to the earlier VESC project.

The VESC met or exceeded 70 of the 82 requirements for the American ESV programme, including air bags instead of safety belts, anti-impact passenger door beams that just made it to the end of the 140/160 series, anti-lock braking (only just introduced on the Jensen FF), pop-up head rests on the seats and an automatic fuel supply cut-off in the event of a heavy accident.

Initially, the 200 series range consisted of a 244 saloon, a 245 estate plus a V6 264 saloon. The 242 two-door saloon seen on foreign markets was not seen in the UK unless privately imported. There were new engines in the smaller four-cylinder cars, and the 264 used the all-new Peugeot-Renault-Volvo 2.7-litre V6 unit. Exteriors were similar to the earlier cars, except that now the front end extended further, making the 244/5 a little longer than the 144/5. The interiors were very similar to the last model year 140/160 series, although further updates were made to the dashboard design. The front suspension was fully revised, too. UK's *Motor* magazine performed an unusual test in 1976, following a Sunday UK press advert stating: "A little moisture in the atmosphere won't stop a Volvo". The local fire

A 244 saloon in its earliest form: the 1974-77 model.

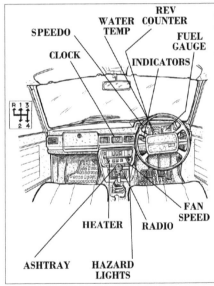

Earliest 200 series dashboard designation. Note square vents replace the round units of the 140/160.

service opened the bonnet of a 244 DL and deployed thousands of gallons of high pressure water to drown the engine. The car then started, much to the delight of the attending Volvo PR men, but three other cars (Mercedes, Golf and Capri) were subjected to the test and all started up, too ...

A 265 V6 estate car derivative joined the

Who let the dogs out? Hunting at dawn with a 245 estate, circa 1980. These rear lamp clusters were updated the following year.

Product crash testing at 35mph with the 245. Volvo takes safety very seriously.

A late 1970s 265 GL. The early V6 engines were refined, but the PRV unit failed to propel them any faster than the four-cylinder 244/5s – and they were less economical to run.

A 264 GL automatic in the Swiss mountains, often called 'dinosaur' due to its looks, with an early 2664cc V6 engine. The first price listed in the UK was £4102 in January 1975, the 164 having only just been deleted.

The round headlamp 1974-1979 design was finished in black; this was a rare 242 GT in correct silver finish with official Volvo fog lamps. The central reflexive bumper inserts were an optional extra on all models. Note bib spoiler.

The second of three saloon boot lids, this one
(1979-1985) on a 242 GT with all the correct
stripes and centre bumper red inserts.

An imported Australian 242 GT shows how easy
entry into the rear is possible with the wide
opening doors. Power was a B23E 2.3-litre.

The front end arrangement shown on this 1979 model 245. USA models by now had unique
Federal round units.

range within a year, as did a DL 264/5 with
cheaper specification and a satin black front
grille on the DL.

In spring of 1977, Volvo built 750 limited
edition right-hand drive pale metallic silver
244s to mark its own 50th anniversary. The
specification included sunroof, tinted glass,
blue synthetic velvet upholstery and a GL
steering wheel. All came with a special 50
year emblem and commemorative silver plate
mounted on the fascia with the signature of
Volvo president Pehr Gyllenhammar. Decorative
gold and black stripes were featured on each
side running just above the rubbing strip but

through the door handles, plus special 'Volvo
1927-1977' oval emblems on front, rear and
both sides. Price was £5325 in manual and
£5595 in automatic form, around £915 more
than the current 244 DL. This specific model
featured as one of Volvo's four classic cars in
a double page advert for the new Volvo 940 in
1990. A 264 Anniversary also existed.

The range continued largely unchanged
until the first major update in late 1978. The
most obvious change was the transition to the
large short-lived square headlamps (although
not in all markets, where round remained due
to local laws) which had headlamp wash/wipe

as standard on the DL and GL models, and these (and the new narrower front grille) were surrounded by attractive chrome strips. The existing large bumper format continued, albeit with a space in the rubber for the front number plate. Other changes included larger more attractive rear lamp clusters on the saloons, and, in addition, the rear boot panel on the saloon was extended 4in down to allow easier loading. Visually it was more pleasing, with the side bump strip extended from the sides and along the base of the revised saloon boot, which now had a more rounded profile on its corner. Exterior mirrors were now finished in black. Seats were revised, and the right-hand model delivered to the UK finally had the wiper blades sweeping the correct way – at long last, the driver had better visibility in heavy rain.

Technical modifications across the 200 range included stiffer springs and uprated dampers, whilst the steering geometry was improved. All cars had a higher compression ratio from this point, whilst fuel-injected models (now badged as GLE) also benefited from a new camshaft and induction, which helped decrease fuel consumption. These changes helped achieve overall sales success for Volvo, with a record 320,000 cars produced

US cars suffered when it came to looks. These models utilised twin small round light units to comply with Federal laws. A late 1970s car.

1981 front lamp arrangement for a 245.

through 1979, when 300 special equipment 244 Thor cars were produced for the UK.

A Volvo Concessionaires-registered 244 GL burns some rubber for a press photo in Ipswich, 1981. Note headlamp wipers.

"For a long time, people have said our cars look like tanks, now we think our latest models really do look like cars," stated chairman of Volvo's UK Concessionaires Dr Jim Maxmin at the unveiling of the 1981 model year range. The headlamps changed again, to rectangular units, and a new front grille was fitted. Taller, more modern wrap-round rear lamp units were utilised on the estate models from late October 1980, as was a small front air dam on the GL and GLE cars, borrowed from the new sporty 2.3-litre GLT launched earlier that year, with matt black bright-work. For the 1981 season the 264/5 B27 V6 Douvrin-built engine was replaced with the larger displacement B28 (from 2664 to 2849cc), obtained by increasing the bore from 88 to 91mm. The entire range now had sills painted black, with plastic mouldings to give a sleeker and thinner appearance, and window surrounds were matt black. The big – and often referred to as ugly – 1974 bumpers finally departed, making way for new aluminium units protected by black cellular plastic, reducing the weight by 26lb (11½kg). Across the range, all models also adopted the new style fascia with easier to reach controls, extra shelving and easier to read instrumentation.

Following UK's Triangle Autos Janspeed 244 Turbo conversion in 1980, in 1981 overseas customers were treated to a 244 Turbo fitted with the standard four-speed gearbox plus overdrive, alloy wheels, front spoiler and stiffer suspension. The Garrett turbocharger gave an extra 26 per cent of power, and torque was up by 45 per cent. In 1980 two Canadians, Gary Sowerby and Ken Langley, broke the world record for driving around the world, taking just 74 days in their Nova Scotia-built 245 DL. The completed journey length was 26,738 miles. The 1980 white estate, nick-named 'Red Car', still survives to this day, and is still driven by the men.

In line with the new 700 series, in late 1982 the models were renumbered: the 244 and 245 became the 240 series, whilst the bigger-engined car became the 260 series, although at this point the saloon version of the 260 was deleted. The 260 GLE estate was now the only Volvo produced with the

By 1982 the model numbers had been redesignated. The 265 became the 260: a V6 car with 2849cc engine and snazzy 25-spoke alloys when brand new.

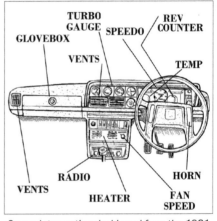

Second generation dashboard from the 1981 model year.

PRV V6, and estates cars trickled off the line for another couple of years seemingly for the UK market only, until disappearing in October 1985 at £12,938. The earlier 244/5 2127cc B21 engine was replaced with the 2315cc B23 unit on all models (it had already been utilised on top line 240 cars), still four-cylinder but with greater performance. Volvo claimed it was an estate car that accelerated faster than a Porsche 924, "When an estate car goes from 0-60mph in just 9.1 seconds, it had better be a Volvo," stated the double-page colour adverts in November 1982, claiming the 240 GLT estate would achieve a top speed of 112mph. The fuel-injected GLT boasted electric front windows, power-assisted

The last type of front grille seen on a 240. This is a 1989 2-litre GL estate with front spoiler and Volvo alloys. Estate sales accounted for 55 per cent of the 240 series.

A 240 GL dashboard from 1989.

steering, electric door mirrors, alloy wheels and central locking. It too had the front air dam. The saloon 244 GLT version was tested by *Autosport* magazine in 1980, achieving that 112mph and an overall fuel consumption of between 22 and 24mpg. The revised front grille was now more vertical, the four-cylinder cars adopted the six-cylinder design bonnet, and the recently revised tail lamp clusters were widened on the saloons.

Diesel versions of the 244 had been available on the continent from 1979 (the

Front aspect of a 240 GL: the last type of bumper, bib spoiler and bonnet pressing.

A January 1991-registered 2.3-litre 240 GLT, one of the last examples built. By now the horizontal rear aspect of the boot had taken on a pronounced curve, exactly matching the rear-mounted spoiler option.

Production of the estates continued later than the saloon: this is a 1992 2-litre 240. Note the extra black finish beneath the side windows and enlarged rear tailgate glass, plus black hinges, tailgate handle and roof rails. Black stripes were also now present along the bottom of the body sides.

fitting of this engine from VW was launched at the Paris Motor Show in late 1978, initially used in DL form only), but in 1983 the VW 2.4-litre six-cylinder diesel engine was offered in GL form in the USA. With air-conditioning, 25-spoke 262C style alloy wheels, tinted glass and velour or leather interior, 29mpg was easily achievable in city driving and 38mpg on the highways. At this point, the US specification cars had rather ugly (to European eyes) twin square headlamps set within the larger oblong area used for European models for the 264/5 models, prior to this in the 1970s, twin circular lights had been fitted in this space, after having deleted the conventional 244 nose cone. The USA also marketed a 127bhp GLT Turbo Wagon estate, with the press release stating "Fast freight, the Swedish way ..."

August 1985 saw another batch of range improvements: the saloon's boot lid took on a more pronounced curve than previously, now matching the contour of the base of the rear window, and a 740/760 style lock plate was fitted. All models got new fronts with revised bonnets, and revised hubcaps were fitted to the wheels. A new style of door mirror was used. An estate car boom in the UK saw the reintroduction of the 240 DL, and along with the 740/760, Volvo dominated the estate car scene, with 43 per cent penetration in the first half of 1986. Its biggest seller was the 240 series, which sold 3638 in that period.

In early 1987, a 240 GLT in manual or automatic was available, with red, white or silver coachwork and black leather upholstery. Fully loaded, it had alloy wheels, electric windows, heated seats and windows, plus low profile tyres. The price range was £10,985 to £12,290. The 240 estate's back end had another major makeover in 1989 when the rear window was enlarged, now de-chromed and more flush with the panel. Together with 1980s style lamp clusters it looked very sleek indeed.

The 240 saloon disappeared from the line-up in 1991, leaving the 240 estate the only remaining 200 series until production stopped in 1993, when nearly 1½ million units had been produced in various factories throughout the world. The final 240 saloons were offered in autumn 1991, with the 240 GL five-speed selling in the UK for £14,300 (2-litre) and £14,660 (2.3-litre). The evergreen estate soldiered on for 24 months in the new car price lists until October 1993 after a 4 per cent price drop, listed at £14,545 (2-litre SE manual) and £14,945 (2.3-litre SE manual). The budget-price limited edition Torslanda estate was offered at £13,995, with around 1000 of these cars imported into the UK in summer 1992, following around 400 the year before. Identified by roof rails and alloy wheels, the Torslandas lost the self-levelling suspension and electric windows of the SE models.

The 260 series rectangular post-1979 headlamps of a 262C. On these, headlamp washers are at the top.

Special-bodied 240/260 cars

Following an earlier factory study based on a special two-door version of the 164, the somewhat unique looking 262C was built by Bertone, and production took place in Turin, northern Italy, with an early example displayed at the Geneva Motor Show in 1977 after what was effectively a top-half re-styling effort from Jan Wilsgaard (Volvo), and some input from Sergio Coggiola (Turin). Overall, around 5622 units were produced as two-door coupés (although some figures suggest 6822 sold worldwide) within the same 2.64m wheelbase, but with a lowered roof line and more steeply raked windscreen and a special leather interior including dark headlining. All cars had a vinyl

The sumptuous leather interior of the 262C. With the roof line 2in lower, room was more restricted, particularly in the rear.

roof with a Bertone emblem on each 'C' pillar, and the mechanics were the same as for the 264 GL. It cost £13,522 – around 60 per cent more than the 264 GL saloon – and the

The 262C Solaire conversion of California looked more like a James Bond villain's ride than something made for an American CEO. Just five are reputed to have been built.

first right-hand drive examples landed on UK shores early in 1979, Volvo planning on 200 to be imported. At the time of writing there are only a handful still registered, according to the website howmanyleft.com. It did not always receive favourable publicity from the media, with one magazine's cheeky artwork department adding a turret on the roof as it felt the car was tank-like. Furthermore, following unfavourable comments about the model, Bertone was reported to have said "It's nothing to do with us, we only make it."

Around three quarters of the 262Cs built were destined for North America, where it replaced the plainer 262 GL saloon (just 3329 of these were produced throughout its short life). That reworked roof was literally given the chop when a handful of Solaire convertible 262Cs were built by Newport Conversions in California. Its main production change was in 1980, when its engine was enlarged from 2664cc to 2849cc (still V6, in-line with the normal 264/265 range of cars), and of course the revised grille, lights and rear boot arrangement described above, before its demise in 1981. Around 6600 were produced.

Whilst the 262C afforded a heavy price increase over the standard 264 GL model, the very long-wheelbase 264 TE was special delivery, and was over double the price of a its donor car. This used the longer 262C front door and specially lengthened rear side door for improved accessibility for any dignitaries. Out of the 335 264 TEs built, just over a third were sold into (then) East Germany, and were a distinct sign of wealth.

The 245T estate (T for Transfer) was based on the same wheelbase as the 264 TE, had three rows of seats, and was popular at international airports, on the school bus run on remote Scandinavian routes, and even with funeral directors. The 5.6m 240 hearse could be specified with two different heights for the coffin area, with a maximum cargo length of 2.35m. Coffins could be easily unloaded with a special sliding tray on silent running rails. It retained standard length front doors, but the lengthened rear side doors of the 264 TE. A factory 245T Express with a high roof would have been interesting, although outside manufacturers quickly produced a

Looking at the clean lines, the mid-section body extension of the 264 TE is not obvious at all.

The 264 TE limousine was an extended 264 GL with added bells and whistles. The extra wheelbase was put to good use on the interior with fold-up central seats.

Another 200 series with extra wheelbase and three rows of seats: the 245T 'Transfer' (circa 1980) that was popular at European airports. Turning circle undisclosed!

240- or 260-based ambulance version both on standard and extended wheelbase cars right through to the 1980s, often with the V6 engine's extra power and sometimes just two side doors. Fuel consumption must have been somewhat alarming!

There are also a number of privately converted pick-ups and custom coachwork cars in various guises seen at modern day car shows. Longer still was the 18ft 2in

Different badges seen on various 200 series cars.

Estate medley. Early and later 1980 rear lamps, rear-facing child seats, and body spacer
inserted above rear side doors (see text). Early models were in body colour, later blackened to
match the door surrounds. The last of the rear lamp clusters in 1979/80 incorporated separate
fog lamps in some markets.

264 Landaulette, built by Bertone. Again a
four-door, but with an extra glazed section
between the front and rear side doors; caution
was certainly needed over hump back bridges
and sharp corners. Before the reunification of

Germany, Fidel Castro of Cuba used one on an
official visit to socialist East Germany in 1984.
After the wall fell an attempt was made to use
the car for advertising sightseeing tours in
Berlin, but it proved unpopular.

240 & 260 series media advertising slogans
A little moisture in the atmosphere won't stop a Volvo (244 DL, 1976)
16.2 years (1976 UK 245 DL estate with 'Long Vehicle' sign on rear bumper)
Why feed 250 horses when you only need 140 (264 GL)
We demand more. We ask less (1979 244 DL)
Art, real estate, gold. And Volvos? (200 series USA, 1980)
Cars people swear by. Not at (200 series USA, 1980)
Bigger is safer, right? Wrong (200 series USA)
Want to buy a performance car, but can you handle the price? (USA 242 GT)
Two ways skiers make tracks with Volvo (USA 242 GT)
You'll probably find it handles better than cars more famous for handling (USA 242 GT)
It takes a lot of dummies to design a car for people who think (244, USA)
At last, an irrational reason to buy a Volvo (USA GLT)
If a car gives you your money's worth, it's not too expensive (USA GLE)
Anyone who's thinking of spending $24,000 for a luxury car should talk to a psychiatrist (USA GLE)
You could drive one years before unloading it (240 estate, USA)
Surely you're not going to let so little stand between you and a Volvo? (244DL, 1981)
Most of the people who buy new Volvos have owned one in the past. The rest are just good at arithmetic – compared to SD1, Granada, BMW 520, Merc 200 (244DL, 1981)
Old Volvos never die, they pass on (USA 240)
Disappointing news for America's 520,000 millionaires, only 1500 Bertone coupés will be offered this year (USA 1980 262C)
Life in the fast lane (USA Turbo)
It can actually make 55mph interesting (USA Turbo)
Fall in love in 6.8 seconds flat (USA Intercooled Turbo)
Fall in love in 9 seconds flat (USA Turbo)
Fall in love in 6.8 seconds flat (USA Intercooled Turbo)
The world's fastest baggage handler? (USA Turbo wagen)
After a few years, most Volvo owners decide to get a better car (200 series, 1983)
Invest in durable goods (USA 240)
The space age vehicle that could transport you into the 21st century (USA 240 estate)
You could drive one years before unloading it (240 estate, USA)
In 2018 AD, while today's Volvos are still roaming the earth, our competition will be an endangered species (USA estate)
What you gain on the swings, you gain on the roundabouts (240, 1983)

240/260 BODY TYPES: two-door and four-door saloons, two-door coupé and five-door estate; **manufactured at:** Kalmar/Torslanda (Sweden), Ghent (Belgium), Halifax (Canada), Melbourne (Australia), Shah Alam (Malaysia), Turin (Italy), Jurong (Singapore), Samut Prakean (Thailand), North Jakarta (Indonesia); **number produced:** 1,483,351 including 6622 262Cs; **production span:** 1974-1992.
PERFORMANCE: top speed: 105mph/170kph (244 GL), 100mph/160kph (265); **0-60mph/100kph:** 11.5 sec (244 GL) 13.5 sec (265); **average economy:** 20-25 mpg (244/5), 19mpg (264).
PRICE AT LAUNCH: £2494-£3275 (244 range), £2790-£3386 (245 range), £3799-£4799 (264 range), £13,522 (262C in 1979).
MEASUREMENTS: length: 16ft 0in (4.88m) in 1974, 15ft 8in (4.78m) from 1981; **width:** 5ft 7in (1.7m); **height:** 4ft 8½in (1.43m), 4ft 7in (1.39m) for 262C; **wheelbase:** 8ft 8in (2.6m); **weight:** 2950lb (1338kg) (244); **wheels:** 14in; **turning circle:** 32ft 3in (9.83m); **fuel capacity:** 13.2 gallons/60 litres; **boot capacity:** 21.7ft^3 (saloon), 71ft^3 (estate).
TECHNICAL: engine types: 1986, 2127, 2315cc four-cyl petrol (240), 2664, 2849cc six-cyl in-line petrol (260), 2383cc (non UK diesel); **gearbox:** four-speed manual/overdrive and later five-speed, three- then four-speed automatic; **suspension:** independent (front) MacPherson struts, coils, anti-roll bar, (rear) live axle, coil springs, Panhard rod; **brakes:** disc front and rear, split diagonally.
TRIM: vinyl, cloth, velour and leather.
KEY OPTIONAL EXTRAS: auxiliary front fog lamps, 3rd row of seats on the estates, tow bar, sunroof, roof rack, self-adhesive bumper stripes, radio cassette, rear headrests, body stripes, electric windows, alloy wheels.

700 SERIES

"Anyone seeking anonymity should avoid this car …" stated a report in *Autocar* with its long-term test 760 GLE in 1983, as it often received disapproving looks from passers by, such was its unique styling. This was a car for the individualist in the early to mid-1980s.

The Project NV80's design had evolved through the late 1970s, and the first of the many prototypes were driven at the factory in January 1978 and shown to management, who helped comment on and finalise the interior design. Unbadged prototypes (save for their Lancia grilles, to throw off the scent those suspecting they were Volvos!) were heat-tested under secret cover later in summer 1978 in both Death Valley, California and the Australian outback, followed by cold weather testing in Sweden and the Italian Alps. The first official glimpse the general public had of anything like the forthcoming new 700 series would have been at the Geneva Motor Show in March 1980, the platform used to display the Jan Wilsgaard-designed VSC (Volvo Safety Car): a vehicle that Volvo considered a serious study, with many safety features built-in that would take its products into the near future.

With its lowered waistline, unlike previous manufacturers' concept cars, this futuristic car genuinely looked like a Volvo product, with a distinctive sloping front grille, enlarged bumpers and boxy appearance. It was lighter than a 245 estate, which enhanced economy and performance; panels were aluminium, and even the tyres were lighter by making use of the Pirelli P8 low-rolling resistance units. It was based on an estate body with the vertical tailgate idea borrowed from the 100 and 200 series, but with a more square and modern American look over the previous 12-year-old design, and featured a few inches of extra roof line opening ahead of the hinges. The large rear lamp clusters were similar to those used on the 740/760 saloons, this entry to the short rear cargo section was over quite a high sill. Compared to the 700 it looked distinctly squat, with a very short rear overhang, but introduced the squared-out wheelarches and side body design of the 740/760. Built-in were unique passive safety belts that moved along

a track when the door was opened, a split 60/40 folding rear seat, cathode-ray electronic display unit, a retractable front spoiler that deployed at speeds over 42mph (70lph) and relocated rear axle arrangement. Power came from the 2127cc four-cylinder engine of the 200 series that was tuned to meet the strict US Californian exhaust emission regulations, and it borrowed its wheels from the 244 GLT. The AiResearch turbocharger fitted came from Garrett. The press enthused about the car when it had been available to test drive a few weeks earlier, and also test drove some LPG-powered 244s at the same time, *Motor* magazine commenting "If this is your idea of fun, Mr Volvo, please could we have more of it?" The prototype still survives in the Volvo museum in Sweden.

Despite Volvo security being exceptionally tight, in spring 1981 news and photos had leaked out of a new luxury top-end saloon model of American design influence into the European motoring press. It was assumed the new Project NV80 (also known later as P31 and then 1155), would be badged as 442, 444, 464 and 465, but the 760, as it became known, was announced in Sweden in early February 1982, albeit slightly late following supply issues from Poland, which had taken some time to set things up.

The first of the production line cars rolled off the lines in October 1981. Initially, just the top-end D28E Douvrin V6 Peugeot-Renault-Volvo engine 760 GLE was offered, with diesel models (turbo and non-turbo, both with a new D24 2.4-litre engine) being built for other overseas and Volvo home markets from early 1983. Surprisingly, the 106mph 760 GLE TD turbo diesel with just manual gearbox option was £1200 dearer than the V6 petrol car. V6 transmission was either three-speed automatic or four-speed manual, both with overdrive. The rear axle was suspended by way of a subframe, reducing road noise.

The Cadillac-inspired North American styling influence seen on the prototype pictures was obvious, with sharp, severe angles and vertical angular lines, plus a near vertical rear window. Another manufacturer that attempted this look was Talbot with its very unsuccessful Tagora model, axed after just a couple of years. The cheaper (even in V6 form) Tagora looked a lot clumsier than the 760. The Volvo was 6in longer than a Granada, but had the added bonus of Boge Nivomat self-levelling rear suspension over the Ford. Compared to the 200 series, the 760 had an extra 5in in the wheelbase, but retained a similar overall length. Rather than aluminium, production panels were pre-zinc-coated steel, allowing thinner 0.7mm pressings to reduced body weight. The luxurious interior was all new, including the fascia. It would be three years later that the 700 series estate version would follow.

The new 760 GLE was exhibited alongside the existing Volvo model range at the March 1982 Geneva Motor Show, with Volvo announcing that it had launched the first car that not only provided ventilation for its passengers, but for its own body, too. Air was taken from the intake in front of the screen and ducted up through the roof and down the pillars and into the sills, where it left through a series of small holes. This helped any long-term corrosion issues that might arise by drying out moisture behind the body panels. Volvo also announced here that ETC (Electronic Traction Control) was to be utilised, which, coupled with VCCT computer control, could also help prevent any wheel-spin. Aerodynamically, the Cd drag coefficient was down to 0.39 from 0.46 on the 264. A press demonstration was to follow in April 1982 in the south of France, followed by another on a UK test track at Chobham, Surrey, which included the (forthcoming to the UK) diesel model.

Around 800 units were destined for the UK market for 1982, mostly as press cars, dealer demonstrators or showroom models (priced at £12,598), all 760 GLE V6s. The existing 260 saloon cars were quickly phased out,

The 760, which was always a V6, available well ahead of the four-cylinder 740 range.

A 760 Turbo intercooler.

The distinctive rear lamp clusters of the new 760 were bigger than any Volvo had used before.

An enthusiastic journalist driving an early 760 GLE in December 1982: this is one of the Ipswich-registered UK press cars. No survival details exist on the DVLA website.

An early production 760 GLE. The new 760s had chrome embellishments around the wheelarches and smart matching alloy wheels.

leaving just the 260 estate model. The home launch price in Sweden was SKr100,000. It was generally agreed that the styling of the new car was an acquired taste, but it did turn heads, with the tail panel receiving the most disapproval.

The 760 GLE was certainly luxurious, and came with, as standard, air-conditioning, manual steel sliding sunroof (electrical operation came slightly later), alloy wheels, leather upholstery, heated front seats, electric windows and central locking. Volvo resisted the temptation to fit the space-age digital instrumentation from the VSS concept car, adopting a more conventional, large and easy to read multi-coloured (mph/kph) analogue control layout with a familiar look, although not the same as the 200 series. Overall, glazed areas were 25 per cent more extensive than on the 244 saloon.

The 760 GLE interior in left-hand drive form.

UK magazine road tests appeared by the end of the autumn, *Autocar* commenting: "Volvo never did have a reputation for producing light, fast and economical cars: quite the contrary, in fact. So it is perhaps no mean achievement that they can offer a fairly big car that competes as well as it does ... If you can live with that striking shape." *Motor* magazine commented on this aspect: "The best thing about the 760's styling is that you can't see it when sitting behind the wheel," but went on: "It's the best car Volvo have

ever made." Volvo's advertising stated "It is a car that turns heads. It is not another bland bullet-shaped offering from some central drawing office." Certainly in the early 1980s world of jelly-mould styling the against-the-tide razor edge 760 made a statement, and it holds up very well, even to this day. As seen on the continent, a cheaper diesel GLE became available in the UK, which quickly became a popular choice on the taxi ranks for a considerable time.

Geneva 1983 show-time again. A new £13,249 760 derivative was displayed with the engine propped up and displayed out of the open bonnet. The fastest production and most

The advert with the copywriter lying under a suspended 740 GL! He trusted the welding strength with his life ...

A 740 GLE with optional body-kit. Visible are the rear spoiler, valence and side skirts. Wind deflectors on the windows and sunroof are fitted, too.

powerful (157bhp) Volvo produced to date, utilising the B23 unit, a four-cylinder 2.3-litre Garrett T03 turbo inter-cooled 760 joined the range which had a claimed top speed of up to 125mph and had a vigorous 0-60mph of around 8.5 seconds. The Turbo had 20bhp more than the larger capacity V6 in the model range, and was offered as the same price as the 760 GLE automatic. The inter-cooler was fitted in front of the standard coolant radiator and the model identified by a small Turbo Inter-cooler motif added to the bottom right hand side of the front grille. Stiffer springs and anti-roll bars were added to the specification; this model followed a 244 Turbo seen overseas, which was not imported as it was not available in right-hand drive form. A marketing campaign compared the 760 Turbo estate to the Porsche 944, where the Volvo could (just) beat the Porsche from 0-60mph.

Due to regulations in the US market, the oblong headlamp unit was not used when the car was launched there some months later, it was replaced by two smaller square headlamp units in the same space which looked clumsy and something of an afterthought. In 1983, over 3000 760s of all types were registered in the UK, whilst for 1984 this increased to over 4000 units sold. Externally, side rubbing strips and wheel trims identified the new five-speed 740 four-cylinder cars from 1984, whilst cloth upholstery and a rather less complex instrument control layout. Using the 240 low friction engines, the Volvo 740 replaced some of the ageing 240 range of cars in the new car price lists, although the 240 was to continue alongside for several years to come. The UK had three new models, a fuel injected 115mph 740 GLT, the carburettor 740 GLE and entry level £9429 740 GL, all with the 2320cc in-line four-cylinder engine. The GLE and GLT came with metallic paint. The near 200kg weight saving gave superior fuel consumption figures over the 760, whilst performance was still impressive with a 0-60mph acceleration figure of 9.4 seconds for the GLT.

Project 1780, the Bertone-styled 780 coupé, stole the limelight at the Geneva Motor Show in March 1985. As with the previous late 1970s 262C, this was an Italian restyled two-door model on the top model once more, and it cost around double the price of a 760 GLE. It has been reported that Volvo stylist Jan Wilsgaard was sent to Turin after some earlier discussions, to help finalise the styling. This plush new P-R-V V6-powered model was available as two-door only, and looked remarkably different to its sister saloon cars with the adoption of a more steeply raked rear screen, with slight BMW 7-series and Maserati overtones. A lowered front grille seemed to suit the car very well, as did the leather trimmed steering wheel and sumptuous interior. There were plenty of bells and whistles inside the car, including wooden trim and electrically operated front seats, which slid automatically forward if the back rest was tipped, to aid

The chairman's choice: 780 Bertone displays its shallower grille. Initially for Italy only in turbo-diesel form, then soon with the V6 PRV engine.

The Bertone-built 780 two-door coupé with its 15-spoke alloy wheels.

The interior of the 780 boasted a well-finished wooden dashboard and expensive sound system. For many years previously, a radio was always an optional extra on a Volvo ...

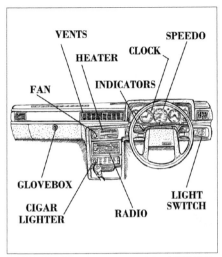

VENTS   SPEEDO

HEATER   CLOCK

FAN   INDICATORS

GLOVEBOX

CIGAR   RADIO   LIGHT SWITCH
LIGHTER

The dashboard designation of the 1987 740 Turbo.

entry to the rear compartment. Exclusive Bertone badges were fitted to the base of the 'C' pillars to preserve the status quo in the director's car park, and it was built left-hand-drive only. Production was undertaken at Carrozzeria Bertone's main Turin factory from 1986 at about 20 a day on a standard 760 floorpan, where all the paintwork, trimming and final assembly was performed, with cars being shipped back to Sweden for final checks before being delivered to dealers. Just over 8500 were built between 1985 and 1990, and very few have been seen in the UK. First deliveries were into Europe, then the USA for the 1987 model year. European specification cars were reputed to have been diesels, either the B230 or turbo B280; others were six-cylinder petrol. To further qualify this new model, Bertone itself was exhibiting the 780 at the Geneva Motor Show, too, alongside a Lamborghini Muira, which was then celebrating 20 years of age.

Barcelona was the May 1985 European public debut platform for the 700 series estate cars, named Ranchera on the Spanish market. From the outset, Volvo had intended to produce saloons, a two-door coupé and estate cars on the 700 platform. The estate had been successfully sold as both 740 and 760 in the North America markets since a US launch at

Chicago and Canadian launch in Toronto three months before, and was built on the same 109in wheelbase. Available from October 1985 in the UK, the interior, with rear sets folded, was cavernous at 75ft³ with a load length of 71½in. The 13.1-gallon (60-litre) fuel tank was a little smaller than that of the saloon, and self-levelling suspension was carried over onto the 760 estate, but was optional on the 740. Unlike the aforementioned VSC safety estate car of 1980, these new estates boasted new reworked vertical rear lamp clusters, which allowed a lower sill for ease of loading. To save weight, the tailgate was aluminium and rose on twin-gas filled struts. It sold alongside the cheaper 240 estate for several years, but the V6 260 estate was by now deleted. A rear facing child seat was offered as a popular option at £349 as was the roller blind load cover at £95.

Both mainstream UK weekly magazines tested the same £16,400 760 Turbo C370TGV, *Autocar* commenting the estates "are better looking than their saloon equivalents …" and *Motor* magazine remarking "the ease with which the driver can deploy the shattering acceleration without any accompanying drama." They affectionately named the car 'Mad Max' with its dark menacing body, tinted glass, black leather seats and aggressive power. The former magazine achieved a one-way best top speed of 128mph, and both achieved a stunning acceleration of 0-60mph in just over 7.5 seconds! In 1985, the UK's Lex Brooklands was also offering Turbo versions of the V6 760, and the factory was building automatic versions, too. Sales were immediately a success, particularly as Ford had stopped making the successful Granada estate, which would have been a major rival, following the introduction of hatchback-only Mk3 Granada.

Volvo went one step beyond with its now-familiar car stack advertisements with the 700 range. Whilst a 740 had been previously used to demonstrate its strength with four cars stacked on top (PV, Amazon, 144 and 164), a new 760 Turbo estate had no fewer than six 760 GLE saloon cars carefully craned into position on it. The picture is featured in this book's introduction.

On the continent, and in the UK from 1986 on, a 760 GLE Executive was an interesting long-wheelbase car with extra room (the extension was 6in/150mm) offered in the rear compartment. In the UK, Avon Coachworks of Royal Leamington Spa, Warwickshire, had offered three lengths for its limousine conversions – 5.09 metres, 5.39 metres and 5.69 metres (the longest with a third row of seats) – with snack trays for rear seat passengers, wood trim and high quality pile carpets. The 760 limousine was shown publicly at the Paris Motor Show that year, the longest vehicle on display. Further conversions existed on the continent by Woodal-Nicholson and Yngve Nilsson, including hearse, limousine and ambulance applications, replacing the now ageing 200 series conversion that had been popular for some time. Often these cars were destined for the DDR, with extra doors, high roofs and flag mountings.

For the 1987 model year came new models that blurred the boundaries between the 740 and 760. Newcomers were the 740 Turbo diesel estate and 740 Turbo (petrol); this model was powered by the same engine as the 760 Turbo, rated at 182hp. The key differences were trim levels and gearboxes: the 760 was automatic, whilst the 740 used manual with overdrive. The larger V6 engine was uprated, too, to produce 170bhp. At this time all petrol engines (except the Turbos) were modified to run on unleaded fuel. To add to the model confusion, the 740 GLT was dropped and the 740 GLE adopted the 131hp petrol engine and overdrive gearbox. High level brake lights were fitted on all 700 series models from this time, and a three-point central safety belt was standard in the rear of all models. Rear-facing child seats could also now be ordered that were fitted on the back of the (folded forward) front seats.

To differentiate the 740 and 760 models to the casual onlooker, a smoother look to the 760 series was announced in late 1987, with models adopting a more rounded nose like (but not the same as) the 780 coupé, and fitment of a lighter aluminium more steeply raked bonnet with a flared rear edge to conceal the windscreen wipers, aid aerodynamics and offer a quieter ride at high speed. The wipers were improved to sweep slightly more of the screen. Changes were also made to the bumpers and front wings, and wider headlamp units now incorporated the auxiliary lights previously fitted below the bumper level. On the 760 saloons, the rear suspension went independent with a split multi-link system, whilst the estates kept the old system to maximise on payload. Underneath, a larger 17.6 gallon petrol tank was fitted. A new, more rounded dash plus four-position adjustable steering column (with new stalks) were fitted inside. Testers preferred the uprated suspension, but found the engine now becoming too long in the tooth. The 740 models continued unchanged in production, at least until late 1989.

In March 1988, Volvo stayed with tradition by again announcing a new model at the Geneva Motor Show. Enter the 16-valve engine fitted in the new 740 GLT. With four valves per cylinder, the new unleaded petrol-only engine came with twin overhead camshafts, with twin counter-rotating balancer shafts to cut down on vibration. The GLT was available as a saloon and an estate version with such models fitted with electric mirrors, windows and sunroof. Also for 1988 – and along the same lines as Ford with its new Mk3 Granada – a fuel-injected 1986cc engine was offered in the Volvo 740 range; this resulted in the car being offered as a tax-saving sub 2-litre model within the company car sector. A limited run 175bhp 780 Turbo was produced from June 1989 identified by its Multi X alloy wheels.

A very expensive 200bhp B204GT-engined 700 Turbo was introduced in selected countries in 1989, being the fastest Volvo ever at the time. This model was not sold in home market Sweden due to its lack of a catalytic converter. A tax-efficient 740 SE entered the UK market at the end of 1989 with a good deal of electric features, and all 700 series cars had front seatbelt pre-tensioners. Turbo models had a revised turbo, which gave a better initial response time, eliminating any turbo lag. An automatic differential lock could be specified as an option for £275, cutting in at up to 25mph if a rear wheel was detected to be spinning.

Another cheeky press advert for the 740

Turbo face-lift appeared in 1990 with the caption "The Volvo 740 Turbo knocks spots off a Jaguar," depicting a four-legged big jaguar cat strolling past a 740 Turbo having shed its spots, with the accompanying script comparing the faster Swedish car to a 2.9 Jaguar XJ6! The 760 series soldiered on with strong sales until late 1990 when it disappeared from the price lists, effectively replaced by the 960 whilst the (2-litre only) 740 came to sales end in 1991 overlapping the new replacement 940 by a few months. Overall nearly a million and a quarter 700 series cars had been built, with 81 per cent of sales going to the four-cylinder. When looking at body types, 32 per cent of sales were estate versions, still often seen in the UK's East Anglia at least, laden to the gunwales being driven by antique dealers ... 700 series rarities also include hearse and ambulance conversions.

The 740 GL estate proved to be a very capable towing vehicle.

The 740/760 estate had a huge load capacity of 75ft^3. This is a 1988 2-litre 740 GL.

A European 740 GLT 16-valve with full body kit at the Volvo Enthusiasts' Club National Rally in 2022.

The clean lines of the 700 series shown on this rear aspect of a 1990 model year 740 GL. Note the later rear lamp clusters.

The 740 was only offered with this revised front end for about a year before its demise, making this 740 GL one of the last built.

A 740 basks in the Spanish sun. Obvious here are the energy-absorbing bumpers.

Two late series cars: the 740 GLT Turbo and 740 GLE estate.

A late series 740 Turbo estate.

700 Series media advertising slogans

At what point does a luxury become a necessity?

The car that took ten years to build

Own a car that will be a comfort to you in its old age (740 GLE)

In the Volvo 760, there is no tourist class

And now for something completely similar (740 compared to 240)

Some status symbols last longer than others (740 GLE)

Just when you thought Christmas was finally over (740 SE)

Don't judge it against the best estate cars, judge it against the best cars

You won't be the first to test drive the new Volvo 740

It's true, isn't it? You always feel better when they drive off in a Volvo

Do something nice for your company. Spend £11,910 on a Volvo (740 GL)

If the welding isn't strong enough, the car will fall on the writer [See photo on page 67]

Will the new 740 uphold the Volvo tradition?

We design every Volvo to look like this (smashed up 740)

If you could test-drive it blindfold, would you guess what car it was?

At last a Volvo designed especially for Mr Lawson

Shouldn't a five figure car have room for five figures?

At Volvo, we think estate cars should be loaded at the back

If we auctioned the Volvo 740 GL, how much would you bid?

How well does your car stand up to heavy traffic? (740 estate)

The clever money is in galvanised steel

Lesson one (740 at London School of Economics))

A Volvo for the executive who likes to drive a hard bargain

The new 760 Turbo: The ultimate Volvo

Own a car that will be a comfort to you in its old age

Quick, which sedan will dust off some of the world's fastest sports cars? (760 Turbo)

"Buy the Volvo" "Buy the world"
You can't go wrong with a Volvo
The only souped-up car that can carry 3988
  cans of soup (740 Turbo estate)
The European luxury car that can survive a
  head-on collision with logic
The future is now
Announcing the arrival of the 16-valve Volvo
  740 GLE. Estimated time of departure:
  Immediately
The BMW 525i is slower, less roomy and costs
  $10,000 more. Maybe it's the new Math (USA
  740 GLE)
The Volvo book of records (760 in stack)
To a radar gun they look exactly alike (USA 740
  Turbo Wagon)
The basic idea behind the Volvo Turbo wagen
A collector's item you can drive everyday (740
  Turbo)
How to survive a mid-life crisis with dignity
  (740 Turbo)
Yes it will fly (740 Turbo)
"I'll park it for you sir"
Introducing some rather unusual competition
  for BMW and Jaguar
Lovely weather for Volvos
Now will you believe us? (customised 740
  Turbo estate)
"Dad, can I borrow the Volvo?"
Obey your instincts. Protect your cubs
Knocks spots off a Jaguar (740 Turbo)
What to do when your family outgrows the
  Lotus (USA 740 Turbo wagon)
For those who would rather be own a fine
  automobile than be owned by one (740 GL)
Buy Volvo. They're boxy but they're good (780)
For those who want something more than a
  Volvo but will accept nothing less (780)
The kind of Volvo you design when you've
  been designing Ferraris, Lamborghinis and
  Maseratis all your life (780)

700 SERIES BODY TYPES: two-door coupé, four-door saloon, five-door estate; **manufactured at:** Gothenburg/Torslanda/ Uddevalla (Sweden), Ghent (Belgium), Clayton (Australia), Turin (Italy), Indonesia; **number produced**: 834,297 saloons, 399,394 estates, 8518 coupés, total 1,242,209; **production span**: 1982-1990.
PERFORMANCE: top speed: 105-125mph/170-200kph;
0-60mph/100kph: 8.3-14 sec; **average economy:** 18-28mpg all model dependant.
PRICE AT LAUNCH: £12,598 (760 GLE saloon).
MEASUREMENTS: length: 15ft 8½in (4.78m); **width:** 5ft 8¾in (1.76m); **height:** 4ft 8½in (1.41m); **wheelbase:** 9ft 1in (2.27m), weight (740 saloon): 2812lb (1272kg) weight (760 estate): 3076lb (1395kg); **wheels:** 15in; **turning circle:** 29ft 3in (8.93m); **fuel capacity:** (four-cyl cars) 13.2 gallons/60 litres, (later six-cyl cars): 17.6 gallons/80 litres; **boot capacity:** 17.1ft^3 (saloon), 75ft^3 (estate).
TECHNICAL: engine types: 1986, 2316cc both four-cyl. petrol, 2849cc six-cyl. in-line petrol, 2383 six-cyl. diesel; **gearbox:** four-speed manual plus overdrive, three-then four-speed automatic; **suspension:** independent coil spring (front), live axle, Panhard rod, coil spring (rear); **brakes:** disc front and rear.
TRIM: cloth, leather.
KEY OPTIONAL EXTRAS: rear facing seats (estate), tow bar, leather upholstery, CD player, sunroof, metallic paint, electronic traction control, ABS, roof rack, dog guard (estate) and £1445 plus VAT bought a cellular mobile phone package in 1986 (included aerial and installation), child seat mounted on back of passenger seat (1986 onwards).

400 SERIES

480 ES

The unique-looking 480 ES Volvo coupé was the third mainstream model built in Holland, following the 66 and then the 300 series. Designed by John de Vries, who won against stiff in-house and Italian competition, it formed part of a successful three car 400 series range built between 1986 and 1996. With front engine and front-wheel drive, this model was a first for Volvo, which was eager to lose its 'slippers and pipe' image.

The 480 came in either fuel-injected or turbocharged forms, powered by the (B18) Renault 1721cc engine and five-speed gearbox, although four-speed automatic versions were available from 1992. A later 2-litre version was non-turbo. An ingenious decision was made to keep the bandolier-style front grille and corporate badge, but this time under the front bumper, thus allowing for a sloping sports image front end, and to circumnavigate NHTSA regulations in headlamp height, pop-up dipped lamps were standard equipment: a first and last for Volvo. Following a bright red example on display at the Geneva Motor Show in March 1986, and many pre-launch scoops, the official launch to an eager press was held in the Haute Savoie region of the French Alps in late April 1986. Motoring hacks learned that the suspension was Lotus-inspired; the running gear French, and Porsche was helping on the design of the future turbocharged version.

A right-hand drive car was displayed on

Cutaway illustration of the new 480 ES coupé. It bore an uncanny resemblance to the Honda Aerodeck coupé. Both What Car? and Motor magazines tested the two together, with both preferring the Swedish car.

The 480 ES undertook some comprehensive safety testing. Much of the front end was plastic, including the bonnet, plus both bumpers.

The pop-up headlamp units were dipped and of the 'follow-me-home' type. Even the door locks were illuminated.

The 480 coupé was made available three years before the mechanically similar 440 saloon version was marketed. It shared the same market as the Reliant Scimitar GTE, which, ironically, had just been dropped.

The 480 ES interior. This was strictly a four-seater. The individual rear seats folded flat and reclined, too. A locking cubby box featured between the rear seats.

Rear aspect of the popular black model. Some media descriptions commented that a car like this from staid Volvo was like your granny wearing a mini skirt!

a rotating platform at the UK Motor Show in October 1986, but there were continuing doubts here as to how fast the new coupé would become available on the UK streets; it was hoped that by mid-1987 every UK dealer would have a demonstration model to sell out the 1500 allocation of cars, but demand was high in domestic Holland and Belgium. It had always been intended to sell 25,000 cars per annum in the very keen US market, but a shift in exchange rates made that unfavourable, and the idea was eventually cancelled in February 1988 a few months after the stock market crash.

In early 1987, news of a forthcoming 480 ES convertible was made public by Volvo's Dutch arm, Volvo Car BV, via the European motoring press, complete with press photos.

Volvo bosses pulled the car at the last minute. The prototype display car proposed for the Amsterdam Motor Show never materialised either, as the Swedish chiefs felt it did not display the correct company image. Design possibilities for an open roof car (the first since the short-lived 1950s P1900) followed for some time, but nothing ever came to fruition, despite it eventually being displayed at the Geneva Motor Show in 1989.

Also in 1989, an eagerly awaited £14,950 turbo version was marketed, complete with extra instrumentation and colour-coded mirrors. Top speed was improved by 10mph to 125mph, and a second was shaved off the 0-60mph time (now 8.5 seconds). Following a showing at the Geneva Motor Show, and alongside the new

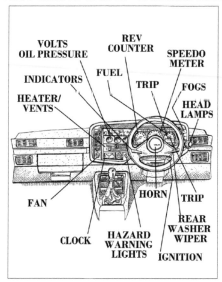

The dashboard binnacle housed a comprehensive array of information. Turbo models had an additional gauge.

Dashboard designation of the 480 ES.

900 series a stunning 480 Turbo convertible design made it to the September 1990 UK Motor Show, too, albeit in two-seater form with a permanent roll bar. The hope was that it would be available the following summer, but this was sadly never the case, as this new cabriolet project was axed following the bankruptcy of a key supplier (Coventry based Motor Panels); several convertible prototypes still survive. From 1991, new style door mirrors were fitted, as were body-coloured bumpers

Rear aspect of the 480 ES. Like the previous P1800, the tailgate was pop-up glass with an aluminium frame, and the wiper operated the moment reverse was selected if the front wipers were already on.

and headrests for the back seats. Due to emissions legislation resulting in a regulatory reduction in power from the 1.7-litre engine, a 2-litre (B20) engine was developed that became available from late 1992 when four-speed automatic transmission was also offered. The cheaper 480 S also joined the range, this came without the alloy wheels, fog lamps and other items seen on the ES and Turbo. A final modification to the 480 before end of production was the adoption of clear indicators at the front plus stronger side intrusion bars.

The 480's reputation was often let down by poor press reports, with long-term test cars that suggested this Dutch-built Volvo was not up to the normal standards of its Swedish cousins. *Motor* (which was taken over by *Autocar* in late 1988) reported on many electrical and gearbox issues, rattling trim and a stalling engine in its 40,000-mile test car, owned from 1987 to 1989, and after selling the car, E77WGK, it remained registered on the road for only another ten years. Despite all the issues, the magazine loved the car.

Limited edition 480s were: 'Paris Blue' (1991) a turquoise model with matching bumpers and leather upholstery; the green and silver metallic 'Two-Tone' with chin spoiler and unique half leather interior (1992); the UK-only 'GT' in metallic racing green or burgundy pearl and air-conditioning (1994); and the 'Celebration' in grey or burgundy metallics or satin white, with special chrome dashboard plaque and CD sound system, crushed leather interior, special alloy wheels and air-conditioning (1995).

A 2.5-litre 170bhp five-cylinder 480 model proposed for 1993 never came to fruition. The 480 left the price lists in July 1995 (the Celebration was listed at £16,500), having sold over 76,000 units. Despite a longer production run, for every eight 440 or 460 cars built, there was just one 480.

480 media advertising slogans
A practical new concept (brochure)
Comfort – a vital factor (brochure)
What makes the Volvo 480 so unique? (brochure)
Coupé 480 ES en route pour le future (France, 1987)

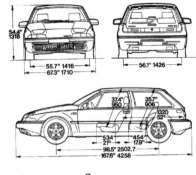
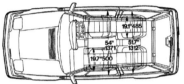

480 ES dimensions.

Free inside every 480, a Volvo
Some people didn't believe it was a Volvo
The Ferrari F40 versus the Volvo 480 Turbo (No, honestly.)
If you can't decide between a sports car and a Volvo, have both
"I'm glad I'm in a Volvo" (480 Turbo)
Peut-etre a-t-elle ete cree pour eprouver votre sagesse ('Perhaps it was created to test your wisdom,' France)
9 seconds suffisent pour passer de la conduit au plaisir ('9 seconds are enough to go from driving to pleasure,' France, 1989, Turbo)
Help beautify your city (translated from Spanish)
Chi lo merita prima o poi diventa Turbo ('Whoever deserves it sooner or later becomes Turbocharged,' Italy, 1988)

Trivia note: for the first time in history, *Autocar* and *Motor* magazines had an almost identical front cover with the same press picture and white background of an ES in November 1985.

480 ES BODY TYPES: two-door coupé (plus some convertible prototypes); **manufactured at**: Born (Netherlands); **number produced**: 76,375; **production span**: 1986-1995.

PERFORMANCE: top speed:
115mph/185kph (non-turbo),
125mph/200kph (turbo); **0-60mph/100kph:**
9.5/8.5 sec (non-turbo/turbo); **average economy:** 26-35mpg.
PRICE AT LAUNCH; £10,850.
MEASUREMENTS: length: 13ft 7½in
(4.59m); **width:** 5ft 6¼in (1.69m); **height:**
4ft 4in (1.32m); **wheelbase:** 8ft 2½in
(2.5m); **weight:** 2140lb (971kg); **wheels:**
14in; **turning circle:** 33ft 3in (10.15m);
fuel capacity: 10.5 gallons/47.7 litres; **boot capacity:** 5.6/23ft³ (seats up/folded).
TECHNICAL: engine types: 1721 and
1998cc four-cyl. petrol; **gearbox:** five-speed
manual, four-speed automatic; **suspension:**
independent front with subframe and
MacPherson struts, rear lightweight constant
track beam axle on coil springs; **brakes:** disc
front and rear, Turbo has ABS, mud flaps,
telescopic antenna, floor mats.
TRIM: cloth and leather faced.
KEY OPTIONAL EXTRAS: leather interior
(£778), air-conditioning, automatic
transmission, roof bars, pop up glass roof, tow
bar, anti-lock brakes.

An early 440 saloon marketing picture. The later CVT automatic version used the steel-band Van Doorne Transmissie gearbox, rather than the earlier single belt 343 system.

440 460 series

The 1994 model year 440 saloon, with a 850-inspired front grille that now lifted as part of the bonnet assembly.

As far back as 1982 there were rumours and
sketches of a new small front-wheel drive
Volvo 500 vehicle (internally codenamed the
G1 then the G15 project) prototypes been
spotted under dusty test conditions in Greece.
Van Doorne CVT transmissions having been
eagerly tested by Fiat on its fleet cars, it
seemed certain something was under way.
Fast forward to an announcement in June
1988: enter the 'timeless' (as Volvo called it)
440 hatchback, which followed the slightly
shorter 480 ES coupé using the same 1721cc
Renault engine in three states of tune (89,
107 and 118bhp) and a manual five-speed
gearbox. The new model was aimed at France,
Sweden, Germany, Italy, Holland and the UK
only. Styling was in-house Volvo (resembling
a kind of off-beat and boxy small 740/760
saloon) after careful consideration of some
Italian proposals. Volvo was quick to point out
the new car was not a replacement for the
existing 300 series, although there was not

much overlap of production. Use was made of
the 480 coupé's floorplan and mechanicals
(and attractive alloy wheels on the 440
GLT and 124mph Turbo variants), and main
production was at the Dutch plant. There were
ongoing legal issues as to the use of the CVT
transmission, so all the models initially offered
were five-speed manual.

The UK range in May 1989 included: GL,
GLi, GLE, GLEi, GLTi and Turbo, all 1.7-litre
(£9795 to £14,595, the top-end 480 Turbo
was £14,950 at this time). A new model 440

The first generation (1991-1993) 460 Turbo with its distinctive chrome grille (see text).

SE arrived in autumn 1990 and sat above the base model but below the GL. By the autumn of 1989 a £9495 base model entered the range for fleet and some private hire applications.

Volvo further widened the 400 series with the 460 in GL and GLE forms (£11,295-£13,395), announced early in 1990 but not immediately available, with an attractive 760-inspired vertical slat grille finished in chrome making a welcome comeback; it added an air of prestige for buyers who preferred this over the black egg-crate grille of the 440. Visually similar to the 440, the 460 was essentially a longer booted version of the mechanically identical 440, and was targeted against the Peugeot 405, Audi 80 and VW Passat. Over the 440, it had slightly narrower rear-quarter windows, a higher boot line and a 4in longer floorplan but within an identical wheelbase. The extra length resulted in a longer boot. It utilised the same 1.7-litre Renault engine, and the range was soon followed by the Turbo, then SE, GLE and plush CD trim specifications by October 1992,

A 440 Turbo model. The 60-0mph braking time was less than 3 seconds ...

Left-hand drive dashboard of the 440 saloon.

The second generation 440 saloon in an idyllic country hotel setting.

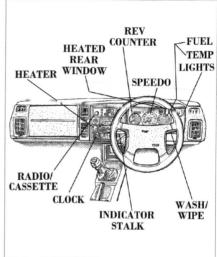

Dashboard designation of the 460.

A 460 Turbo. This model had 120bhp and a top speed of 124mph.

The booted Volvo 460 GLE injection. Popular with owners who did not want to let rain in (or heat out) as with the 440 hatch.

offered with new 1.8- and 2-litre engines. The 440 benefited from these engines, too, with no CD, but a GLT being offered. The top model

460 Turbo cost £15,995 (the 440 Turbo was £15,095 at this time) and lasted until 1992, and was reinstated later.

From September 1993 a common across-the-range style 850-inspired grille replaced the earlier types on both 440 and 460 and now formed part of the bonnet. Headlamps went slimmer, and bumpers were redesigned complete with integral spoiler. There were more rounded lamp units fitted at the rear, also 850-inspired. New style alloy wheels were also fitted, along with revised door mirrors. Interiors were updated, too; new materials including a combination of cloth and leather, there were reshaped seats, and some switchgear was moved – window and mirror switches were now door-mounted. The driver's seat got an airbag, the passenger went without.

From July 1994, a (reworked Renault 19) 93bhp 1.9-litre turbo diesel engine was finally offered in the 440 (briefly) and 460, with an extensive advertising programme. A new steel CVT belt system was fitted to newly available HTA 'High Tech Automatic' automatic cars (option cost £795 on 1.8-litre petrol cars only). By November 1994, the 440 range had been deleted from the new UK price lists, leaving just the 480 coupé and 460 with its 15 model line-up; 1.6i, 1.8i, 2.0i, 1.9 TD also Si, the

1.7i Turbo, but the SE was replaced by Si, and the CD was still top specification car.

In summer 1995, further 460s were available on top of the existing range: Family, Sport, Business, Performance and Luxury. These came in various trim guises, the dearest being 460 Luxury CD Turbo at £16,650. Finally, from the end of 1995, the 460 ES replaced SE badged cars, and by the middle of 1996, the 460 range was just base, 1.9TD, S, LE, GS and CD, with diesels available with all trims types except CD. By October 1996 the 460 had vanished, having been replaced by the brand new S40 saloon earlier in the year. The £16,845 460 2.0 GS was the dearest car in the range at the demise.

440/460 media advertising slogans

We can't say how long a used Volvo will last. We've only been making them for 68 years.
The olive is merely an appetiser (440 ES)
...this car has been crashed, baked, frozen, driven mercilessly for a million miles... Well, what do you expect for £9,940?
Will a Volvo's safety cage allow it to drive through six brick walls?
For £9,970 the Volvo will look after you. (For £0,000 he'll look after the Volvo)
The government spends over £2.4 billion every year making Britain's roads safer. You can do it for just £9,695
More turbo than diesel
Fuel-injection, sports handling and flat out all the way (440)
The car that changes the rules (440 TV advert)
£9,970 service included (440, 1994)
£9,990 will buy you a less vulnerable cage (440)
It's true, you are better protected with a Volvo (440)
The Volvo 440, from £9,695 upwards (stack advert)
With the Volvo 440 you won't burn up on re-entry
The steering wheel is not just for holding the airbag (440)
Nous vous avons regarde aimer. Et nous avons cree la Volvo 440 ('We've watched you love it. And we created the Volvo 440,' France, 1988)

Dix petits kilos, a transporter sont parfois une lourde resposabilite ('Carrying ten small kilos can be a heavy responsibility.' France 1988, 440)
Nouvelle 460 Volvo. L'automobile commence une nouvelle vie ('New 460 Volvo. The automobile begins a new life,' France, 1990)
L'ete sera chaud (mais pas dans les Volvo) ('Summer will be hot (but not in the Volvos)' France, 1993)
Un jour ou L'autre, on decide de se soucier de son environnement ('One day or another, we decide to take care of our environment,' France, 1990 460)
Il n'y a pas que la securitie dans la vie ('There's more to life than safety,' France, 400 Turbo diesel)

440 460 BODY TYPES: (440) five-door hatch and four-door saloon (460); **manufactured at:** Born (Netherlands); **number produced:** 609,815; **production span:** (440) 1989-1994, (460) 1990-1996.
PERFORMANCE: top speed: 108mph/175kph; **0-60mph/100kph:** 12.5 sec; **average economy:** 27-35mpg (1.7-litre 440).
PRICE AT LAUNCH: £11,495 (440 GLE), £15,995 460 Turbo.
MEASUREMENTS: length: 14ft 1¾in (4.31m); **width:** 5ft 5¾in (1.67m); **height:** 4ft 7¼in (1.41m); **wheelbase:** 8ft 2½in (2.5m); **weight:** 2154lb (977kg); **wheels:** 14in; **turning circle:** 33ft 3in (3.2m); **fuel capacity:** 10.6 gallons/48 litres (440), 13.2 gallons/60 litres (460); **boot capacity:** 16ft³.
TECHNICAL: engine types: 1596, 1721, 1794 and 1998cc all four-cyl. petrol, 1870cc four-cyl. diesel; **gearbox:** five-speed manual, four-speed automatic; **suspension:** independent MacPherson struts with coils, rear beam axle with Watts linkage coil springs; **brakes:** disc front and drum rear.
TRIM: cloth, leather.
KEY OPTIONAL EXTRAS: automatic transmission, steel belt CVT automatic transmission, plush leather or leather faced seating, ABS and TRACS, air-conditioning, fog lights, heated seats, 14 and 15in alloy wheels, metallic paint.

900 SERIES

The 740 and 760 range had seen various production changes throughout its sales life of eight years, and the two models suffered an identity crisis towards the end of production, with a confusing range of engines often available in either vehicle. The 760 had a major face-lift in autumn 1987, which was not followed by the 740 for some time. The whole range was in need of an update: the angular looks were still not to everyone's taste, particularly the saloon, and the six-cylinder engine of the 760 was getting rather long in the tooth. The truth was the 940 and 960 cars were a major refresh of the previous 700s, but to punctuate this, Volvo announced this next face-lift by way of an entirely new range with new model numbers, namely 940 for the four-cylinder cars and 960 for the six-cylinder cars.

Of course, there were quite a few detail changes to these new cars that were announced in September 1990 and made their world debut at the Birmingham NEC Motor Show in the UK. Confusingly, although the 760 was dropped immediately, the 740 continued in both saloon and estate form; indeed, a 740 estate was featured alongside the new 940 and 960 at the UK show, along with a splendid 480 ES convertible that never made it to production. The most noticeable change was the revised rear end of the saloon,

Early production 940 saloon.

The 940 estate had the same load carrying capacity as the 700 series: 75ft³.

which employed a less steeply angled rear screen, which in turn gave a slightly enlarged rear quarterlight and higher boot line. New rear light clusters were employed and a new

A 940 saloon with colour-keyed bumpers.

European street scene with a late series 940 saloon.

rear bumper, and overall the drag co-efficient was improved from Cd 0.40 to Cd 0.36. The styling changes allowed for an extra 20mm of headroom in the rear compartment, whilst the boot gained an impressive 120mm in available height. However, taller drivers found themselves looking through the windscreen's tinted shade-band even with the adjustable seat at its lowest point. The central rear armrest now cleverly doubled as a child seat with its own three-point safety belt.

What attracted the most attention was the utilisation of the Porsche-inspired all alloy 2.9-litre six-cylinder engine for the 960 when ordered in top specification. With 24 valves and 204bhp it was good for 130mph. Developed by Volvo from the PCP (Power Concept Project), Porsche had been engaged as a consultant to help with the tuning aspects, including the Motronic direct (coils fitted on top of the sparkplugs) ignition and injection system. The new B6304F 2922cc engine carried 11 new patents. Similar in use to the big Opel and Vauxhall Senator rival cars from GM, the electronically managed four-speed automatic gearbox could be used

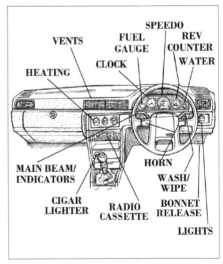

The 940 SE dashboard designation.

in either 'Sport', 'Economy' or 'Winter' mode. This gearbox had been developed by the Japanese company Aisin-Warner, which also supplied Toyota/Lexus. Like some later 700s, there was also an electronically-controlled limited-slip differential. A three-way catalytic converter was fitted with a Lamda Sond probe, with a badge on the front grille to reflect this.

The 960 could also be bought with a 2.0 litre turbocharged engine (there were no 24v badges to identify the faster car with its less expensive stable-mate), whilst the 940 came in fuel-injection 2.3-litre GL or GLE form, or 2-litre GL or SE only. For a £1200 saving over the 960, a 940 2.3 Turbo was also offered. Of course, the ubiquitous diesel completed the model line-up, in 940 guise.

Double-page adverts for the £19,100 940 GLE appeared in the motoring press and Sunday papers, featuring key historical Volvo models through the years, and boasting that the new 940 was the quietest Volvo ever made, with an extra 11 sound-dampening panels in the rear. The large format preview brochure also concentrated heavily on Volvo history. The new 940 model still retained the older rear suspension setup brought over from the 740, with a solid rear axle arrangement. Volvo said that most American buyers (a major market) would not notice the difference! The 960 utilised the newer 760 rear suspension setup, introduced a couple of years earlier. The complete range of prices in October 1990 included £15,900 for the 940 2.0 GL to £28,200 for the 960 3.0 24v estate.

Throughout the lifespan of the 900 series, road testers generally criticised the "slab-like out-moded interior" and "complete lack of chic" (*What Car?* on a used car test). In its 1990 road test of the 24v, *Autocar* reported that it was "Volvo's best executive saloon so far," remarking that it was the fastest (top speed) Volvo it had ever tested, and praising the new engine.

In March 1991, to join the existing 2.3-litre 740 Turbo, and squeezing in under the UK tax budget came the 2-litre 124mph 940 SE Turbo. Its only distinguishing internal feature was a turbo boost dial in the instrument binnacle. The model cost an extra £870 but was no tarmac scorcher, although a couple of seconds quicker to 60mph over the standard car was achievable, as was an extra 10-15mph top speed (now 126mph). The small fast-spinning turbocharger and relatively low

boost pressure meant that the emphasis was on a strong response in mid-speed range and minimal delays after depressing the throttle when coming on boost. The tempting "Who says power corrupts?" UK double-page press advert ended with the line: "'Power', as Henry Kissinger put it, 'is the ultimate aphrodisiac.'"

In 1992, a base model 940S was added to the range and the non-turbo 940 SE was deleted. This entry level 940S model featured manually operated windows and non-electric door mirrors, but retained most of the SE specification. At the same time, all models received the SIPS side-impact protection system and anti-lock brakes. A top level 960 Executive saloon was added to the range by the end of 1992 with a high specification of equipment, retailing at £11,000 more (a 40 per cent increase!) than the standard 24v 960 at £37,350. The 24v 960 estate was now £27,195. For those who were retail price conscious, the Wentworth estate, based on the 940 Turbo but with air-conditioning rather than a sunroof – plus all the bells and whistles – was also available until the 1994 improvements. It did not carry 940 badges and could easily have passed as a 700 series from the back. The 2.3 Turbo 960 was dropped by this point.

Following criticisms that the 900 series had largely retained the 1980s interior from the 700 series, a new softer dash with more user-friendly switchgear was featured from late 1994 with better switches, but it still looked very similar to the previous one, save for optional different trim colours. New curvaceous door trims were fitted, as was a new restyled steering wheel. A face-lift was evident, with softer lines, body-coloured bumpers and thinner headlamps, bringing the car in-line with competitors such as the new Omega. By this time ITN, a UK television news broadcaster, had a 49 strong fleet of 940 estate cars to travel the country coast to coast, and often Europe, for that elusive news story.

The 960 was also available with a new high-revving (6500rpm) 170bhp 2.5-litre six-cylinder engine, a de-stroked and sleeved-down version of the 3-litre 24v. It came in either four-speed automatic or five-speed

A later series 940 estate with 20-spoke alloy wheels.

A well-kept 1994 2-litre Wentworth saloon.

The same Wentworth partially displaying a leather interior and automatic transmission.

A Volvo 960 poses in the Italian Alps.

The 960 estate.

manual format. There were also five new specification levels and three internal colour options which really opened up the 960 range.

Power steering improvements now gave 3.5 turns lock-to-lock with heavier weighting for improved feedback. The rear suspension

A 960 estate, rear aspect. From this angle, it was almost identical to the 760 estate.

A later 960 saloon.

came under change, too, with the state also receiving the revised, and smaller, rear multi-link arrangement. Although it sounds like a backward to step to 1960s Triumph Herald times, weight advantages of 11kg were also gained by replacing the coil springs with a transverse leaf spring housed between the wheels and half-shafts; this all resulted in a massive improvement in handling and ride. Front suspension was brought in-line, too, to

match the 850, which helped to reduce body roll on heavy cornering.

By March 1995, the 940 2.3 LPT estate was fitted with a low pressure turbo, but its discreet extra performance was not enough to smoke the tyres. Overall torque was improved, the modest extra 19bhp gave a handy lag-free 170lbft at just 2300rpm, ideal for towing, but the road testers were still complaining about the "ergonomic-disaster" dashboard, citing the

The 960 Luxury Edition poses in Marlow, UK.

The 960 Luxury Edition, interior aspect.

Sumptuous interior of the 960. Headrests are now solid, leaving behind the 1970s image.

850 2.0 SE as a better buy at £910 more. In December 1995 further improvements were made to the side impact protection bars, seat-mounted side air-bags were fitted, a remote anti-theft alarm was fitted to the 960, and the diesel engine's displacement was increased to 2.4-litre.

Knocking on the doors of the Rover (Sterling) and the Vauxhall/Opel (Omega Elite) as a final run out 960 model, in March 1996 the 960 Luxury Edition (in 2.5 SE, 2.5 CD and £28,500 3.0 CD form) was announced which offered a substantial list of 'extras' at a competitive price. The top specification included air-conditioning, a colour co-ordinated spoiler, leather upholstery, 16in 15-spoke alloy wheels and full wood trim treatment. Later in 1996 saw the Torslanda name re-appear on a budget estate, this time the 940 costing £16,515. It included a healthy specification including SIPS and ABS plus headlamp wash/wipe.

Reminiscent of the now-deleted 240 Torslanda estate of 1992, an entry level 940 estate was marketed from late 1996. Also at this time, an exclusive additional saloon, the expensive 960/S90 Executive (the 'Royal' in certain markets), was aimed at business users on the move and had an extra 6in (150mm) in its wheelbase and reworked 'C' pillars for added privacy. The option for a small office printer and a cooling box were available in the rear centre seat (no child seat!), and air-conditioning could be operated separately. Interior lighting was uprated, too, as was the sumptuous seating; the rear seat squabs were 2in (50mm) longer, and the car could be ordered with just four seats rather than five, in which case each of the rear pair could

The S90 was available from 1997 model year, and was essentially a face-lifted 940/960.

be adjusted electrically, including fore and aft movement. A retractable rear sun blind completed the privacy experience.

The 940 and 960 continued largely unchanged until their demise: in March 1998 for the 940, whereas the 960 was renumbered S90 (saloon) and V90 (estate) for the 1997 and (brief) 1998 model years from March 1997. It was deleted from the price lists in April 1998. The run-out 940 Classic ended up available in many guises, making the specific choice for a buyer very comprehensive: there were sixteen body colours, with a choice of three types of alloy wheel, 15in Adhara or Pholus, plus stylish 16in Auriga wheels, some seven internal trim types and a choice of power, the 2.3-litre petrol engine in light pressure or high power turbo forms. Badges trim specifications were Classic, Standard Equipment, SE and CD, and an optional 'Sports Pack' included

lowered suspension, uprated shock absorbers, locking differential and blacked out sports grille plus rear spoiler. The 'Estate Pack' could be ordered on such models, which provided load compensating suspension, roof rails and a rear luggage guard for dogs or parcels. The 900 series demise was the last Volvo would see of rear-wheel drive cars.

The end of run prices in March 1998 for the 940 range were:

940 2.3t Classic saloon £18,255, estate £19,355
940 2.3t SE saloon £19705, estate £20,805
940 2.3t CD saloon £21,805, estate £22,905

The rebadged 960, which had confusingly become the S90 saloon and V90 estate, lasted another month on the lists until April 1998 after production stopped on 5th February 1998:

960 3.0 24v auto V90 estate type only
£25,005
960 3.0 24v SE S90 saloon £26,255, V90
estate £27,255
960 3.0 24v CD S90 saloon £28,755, V90
estate £29,755
960 3.0 24v Luxury S90 saloon £28,355
V90 estate £29,355
960 3.0 24v Executive S90 saloon type only
£32,155

Note that the S90 and V90 model names
returned on a completely different car in 2016.

Nillson/Volvo produced some long-
wheelbase executive limousines based on
the 960, with some exported to USA. There
were also plenty of 960 derived ambulance
conversions, many with bespoke bodywork
with a variety of roof heights, door options
and wheelbases. Often these went through
a lengthy build process and some were
registered well after the demise of the 900
series.

940/960 media advertising slogans

*Where the pursuit of excellence inevitably
leads you (940)*
*You don't have to crash this Volvo to
appreciate its beauty (940)*
*You can't go wrong with a Volvo (1992 940
GL)*
*Who says power corrupts? (1991 940 2.0 SE
Turbo)*
*How to improve a Golf's turning circle (940
estate)**
Not bad for your first car (940 Turbo estate)
*You don't have to crash this Volvo to
appreciate its beauty (940 saloon)*
*All this for £19,245. Only the Wentworth could
carry it off (estate)*
*For families who've grown too big for their
boots (940 GLE estate, Australia)*
There's more to it than meets the eye (960)
Yes it is a Volvo (960)
*Compromise shouldn't enter your vocabulary,
let alone your garage (960)*
*These days, there's only one way to justify
$45,00 for an automobile. Spend £34,500
for it (960 in USA)*
The latest in a long line of firsts (960)

*We changed everything but our philosophy
(960)*
*At Volvo, we never cut corners, but who says
you can't cut round them (960 USA)*

*Hailing back to the stacked car advert
theme again, perhaps the author's favourite
from the above list was a VW Golf carefully
perched on top of a 940 estate, the copy
cheekily suggesting that the large Swedish car
had a better turning circle than the smaller
German one. It was devised by UK advertising
agency Abbott Mead Vickers.

900 SERIES BODY TYPES: four-door
saloon, five-door estate; **manufactured
at:** Gothenburg/ Torslanda and Kalmar
(Sweden), Ghent (Belgium), Halifax (Canada),
Samutprakam (Indonesia); **number produced:**
1,530,000; **production span:** 1990-1998.
PERFORMANCE: top speed:
120mph/195kph, 130mph/210kph (960);
0-60mph/100kph: 12.2/9.0 sec (940/960);
average economy: 20-30mpg (model
dependant).
PRICE AT LAUNCH: £15,900 (940), £26,950
(960 24v).
MEASUREMENTS: length saloon: 15ft 11½in
(4.87m), length estate: 15ft 8½in (4.84m);
width: 5ft 8¾in (1.75m), height saloon:
4ft 7½in (1.41m), height estate: 4ft 8½in
(1.43m); **wheelbase:** 9ft 1in (2.77m); **weight:**
2860-3300lb (1300-1500kg; **wheels:**
15/16in; **turning circle:** 32ft 2in (9.9m);
fuel capacity: 16½ gallons/75 litres; **boot
capacity:** 17ft^3 (saloon), 75ft^3 (estate).
TECHNICAL: engine types: 1986 and
2316cc four-cyl petrol, 2473 and 2922cc
six-cyl petrol, 2383cc six-cyl diesel; **gearbox:**
four-speed manual, five-speed; **suspension:**
independent coil, rear self-levelling (on 960)
telescopic dampers, coil; **brakes:** disc front
(ventilated) and rear.
TRIM: cloth and leather.
KEY OPTIONAL EXTRAS: load compensating
suspension, locking rear differential, air-
conditioning, cruise control, plush leather or
leather faced seats, CD autochanger, towbar,
16in alloy wheels, black paint.

850 SERIES & S70/V70

The first news of the new 850 saloon model arrived in spring of 1991, with the first UK deliveries arriving May 1992. The 850 was seen as a direct replacement to the ageing 200 series and offered a new design, with more rounded body panels, which was to set the way forward for Volvo in future years. It sat firmly between the new 900 series and the smaller 440 and 460 saloons, and was built in a variety of factories worldwide. Initially front-wheel drive only, an all-wheel-drive estate version arrived towards the end of production. The 850 became available from summer 1992 in North America, and lasted in all markets until the end of 1996, when replaced by the S70 and V70 models –

outside the scope of this publication, albeit a mild face-lift of the 850.

A humble model line-up was available at the start of production, saloons only, in 5v two- or five-cylinder 2.5-litre GLT format which lasted four years. The following year brought in the cheaper 2-litre SE version, and the range widened further still in June 1993 with the 850 estate model. It featured bumper to roof tail-lamp clusters, with twin bulb feature top and bottom. Designed by Rolf Malmgren it immediately proved popular with business users, families and the antique set. It boasted 56ft^3 boot capacity, not quite that of the larger estates, but nevertheless very useable, with advertising stating that it could carry a plethora of goods including sail boards, 120 traffic cones and full-size Cameron hot air balloon!

A 1995 850 2.5-litre estate. Load capacity was 56ft^3 with the rear seats down; just slightly less than the larger 700 and 900 series.

The five-cylinder 20-valve engine of the 850.

Comprehensive crash testing at 35mph.

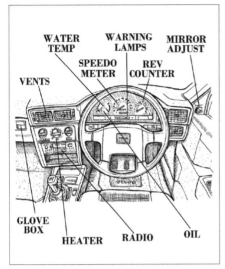

Dashboard designation of the 850.

Front aspect of the high performance T-5R. This colour was certainly striking; ironically very similar to the slightly later and less exciting Fiat Panda!

Rear aspect of the T-5R saloon, with its distinctive boot-mounted spoiler.

In October 1993 there were further changes and additions with a 10v engine option on the cheaper models and a stunning £23,995 2.3-litre T5 Turbo saloon and estate. *Auto Express* magazine commented "Ultimately, it's the mind-blowing performance that really sticks in our mind," with Volvo hype advertising 0-60mph in 6.7 seconds and 150mph. By spring of the following year,

Volvo was showing a mock-up race car in full BTCC livery at the Stockholm Motor Show, but remained tight-lipped about its future. Of course, Volvo made headline news in 1994 when it entered 850 estate cars in the British Touring Car Championship, and saloons in 1995.

During 1994, both bumpers were updated, as were, very subtly, the headlamps

The T-5R was also sold as an estate and heavily marketed in the media. Top speed was over 150mph, with a 0-60mph time a shade under 7 seconds: all for rapid antique delivery, of course ...

Rear aspect of a 1996 850 T-5.

and indicators, and a new switchgear was introduced inside. Dwarfing the new cheaper S and GLE models introduced at the same time, the October 1994 launched T-5R (which replaced the T5), made its debut as a special edition. An early production left-hand drive yellow T-5R estate was driven from Sweden by *Top Gear* magazine journalists so the stunning new model could star at the October 1994 UK

Motor Show. Their aim was to achieve a flat-out run on the German autobahn, but this was thwarted by poor weather and heavy traffic. When tested, it matched the performance of the T5 Turbo. Originally set at just 50, but then 200 cars entered the UK in 1995, either in an odd choice of cream yellow or jet black. Worldwide sales were over 5000. The distinctive 17in gunpowder six-spoke alloy

Front aspect of an 850 T-5. Passing in the background is a later C70.

The additional folding child seat was cleverly located in between the rear seats.

Comprehensive dashboard of the 850.

wheels were almost shelved by Volvo bosses as being too aggressive, but fortunately kept on-board. Even toy manufacturers Hot Wheels made a model ... Then, for an extra £4000,

the even hotter 850R replaced the T-5R. At 250bhp and 259lb/ft torque, it was advertised with a top speed of 155mph (where legally possible). To prevent wheelspin, electronic traction control and a viscous coupling were fitted. Volvo advertising stated: "If power is the ultimate aphrodisiac, prepare to be seduced." It ran until the S70/V70 took over at the end of 1996. In December 1995, the lavishly equipped 850 CD was added to the range, and the existing 2461cc Audi A6 turbo diesel engine was utilised for the range by turning the motor by 90 degrees and squeezing it under the bonnet. Cost was from £21,000 and a creditable 64mpg achievement (at 56mph) was possible if careful, with a possible 125mph top speed.

May 1996 saw the announcement of an all-wheel drive 850, badged as the 850 AWD, and available in estate form only within a few months. Appealing to the country set with its full-length roof rails, this £27,400 load hauler came with part leather interior wood veneer dashboard and 2.5 litres with 193bhp. Most of the time it was 95 per cent front-wheel drive, with a TRACS liquid silicon automatically expanding when required, so the viscous coupling transferred power to the rear under wheelspin conditions. Under braking, drive to the rear disconnected altogether for improved stability. Fuel consumption suffered a little, road testers generally achieving 19mpg overall. The Volvo 850 lasted until December 1996 when the range was effectively rebadged as the S70 (saloon) and

The 850-R AWD brought all-wheel-drive transmission to the range quite late on in production. It came with TRACS traction control, too.

The later S70 saloon/V70 estate replaced the 850 with a front-end face-lift and many other modifications, including the C70 coupé dashboard. This is the V70R ...

V70 (estate), and received a front end face-lift. The rear screen of the saloon was less sharply raked resulting in a new boot lid, with an interior refresh and a total of 1800 other changes. The S70 and V70 continued (without the T-5R), largely unchanged for a further three years, with the saloon now getting the AWD option to match the estate in 1998, although UK sales were in the hundreds, not thousands.

... whilst the later S70 saloon replaced the 850 saloon. They both ran from 1996 to 2000.

850 media advertising slogans

In a 40mph bend the suspension is unparalleled
You can't go wrong with a Volvo
No wonder it corners so well
Some comparisons are too hard to bear
You can't tell it's an estate until you see the back of it
This is not your uncle Olaf's Volvo (850 GLT)
History repeats itself (850 GLT)
Just when you thought you knew everything about Volvo (850 GLT)
If you think you know about cars, try matching the quotes (T-5)
What on earth did they put in the herring over there? (T-5R)
We're not trying to sell you this car. We're just letting you know it exists (T-5R)
New touring cars from Volvo (850 CD)
Put more excitement into your driving! (1995)
4x4 = 850 (1996)
An incredible rate of knots (850 Turbo diesel)
After years of building cages, we are about to let the animal out (850 R)
If power is the ultimate aphrodisiac, prepare to be seduced (850 R)
Saturday morning errands will never be the same (estate)
Volvo's wilder child (ASTC estate racer, Australia)
First across the line for safety (BTCC)
With 56ft³ of load space, there's more than enough room for a trophy or two (BTCC)

850 V70/S70 BODY TYPES: four-door saloon, five-door estate; **manufactured at**: Torslanda (Sweden), Ghent (Belgium), Halifax (Canada), North Jakarta (Indonesia), Santa Rosa (Philippines); **number produced**: 1,360,522; **production span**: 1991-1999.

PERFORMANCE: top speed: 120mph/195kph (2-litre) to 155mph/250kph (850R); **0-60mph/100kph**: 10 sec (2-litre) to 6.7 sec (850R); **average economy**: 20-35mpg (petrol models, diesels were better).

PRICE AT LAUNCH: £18,925 (1992 2.0 GLT) to £32,425 (1996 850R).

MEASUREMENTS: length: 15ft 3½in (4.66m) (saloon), 15ft 5½in (4.71m) (estate); **width**: 5ft 9¼in (1.76m); **height**: 4ft 7½in (1.41m); **wheelbase**: 8ft 9in (2.66m); **weight**: 3053-3351lb (1385-1520kg) (saloon), 3230-3461lb (1465-1570kg) (estate); **wheels**: 15in (17in R and T-5R); **turning circle**: 33ft 6in (10.2m); **fuel capacity**: 16 gallons/73 litres; **boot capacity**: 15/56ft³ (saloon/estate, seats down).

TECHNICAL: engine types: 1984, 2319, 2435 and 2473cc all five-cyl. petrol, 2461cc five-cyl. diesels; **gearbox**: five-speed manual, automatic; **suspension**: coils at front with lower wishbones, multi-link axle with coils at rear; **brakes**: disc front and rear, ABS brakes. **TRIM**: cloth, leather.

KEY OPTIONAL EXTRAS: load compensating suspension, rear boot spoiler, 16in alloy wheels, leather upholstery, air-conditioning (replaced sunroof), roof rails, electric glass sunroof, burr walnut dash, towbar, traction control.

APPENDIX 1 – COMMERCIAL & MILITARY VEHICLES

Volvo is recognised for its medium- and large-scale commercial vehicle production, but some car based models have been adapted for commercial use straight from the production line. The Duett vans, based on both types of PV and designated PV445 and P210 respectively, were popular in the 1950s and 1960s (see descriptions within the first two chapters), with the initial PV445 overlapping the production of the new PV544 by a couple of years. There were pick-ups, ambulances, panel vans and plenty of bespoke conversions that saw reliable service initially in Europe, then when production opened up, the rest of the world.

Although strictly not Volvo, the Daf car range was also produced as a micro panel van with its easy forward-reverse gear lever and Variomatic transmission, just right for city deliveries. The author remembers being a child passenger in an Essex meat van delivering at dawn with father, and often driving this on private land! Whilst the Amazon platform saw some ambulance conversions, when the range was mothballed a new 145 estate lent itself well to a commercial

A kitted out P210 panel van in use by the Swedish Telecommunications in Sweden in familiar orange livery. Note extra side window to help visibility at road junctions.

application by way of the 145 Express, a high roof version with front-mounted roof rack that also did service as an urban taxi in remote areas. This standard specification model continued with the early 140 style grille and overlapped the new refreshed 140s in the early 1970s. No 240 Express version existed, but, as with the 700 and 900 series, long-wheelbase commercial applications were built, including more ambulances, leaving the path open to limousines and state vehicles, too.

A 1955 PV445 pick-up with some modern customisation, seen on the Volvo Enthusiasts' Club stand at a Suffolk vehicle gathering in 2022.

The 1970s commercial C300 series cross-country truck sometimes made its way to UK shores, with a petrol 3-litre straight-six engine of the previous 164 series, and selectable four-wheel drive and low gear ratio option. Production was in Romania, with a total of

The 1974 TGB1111 military vehicle flies the Swedish flag. Power was from a 164-style six-cylinder engine.

8718 built 1974-1984 (C303, 304 and 305). Just before production ended, the C303 went on to win the Light Truck Class in the gruelling 1983 Paris-Dakar Rally. With its enormous ground clearance and massive off road tyres (it resembled a Steyr Puch Pinzgauer), it was designed for a Swedish Defence Forces contract, and the military was soon to place an order. The eye-catching TGB1111 (based on the C303) seen in this section, photographed in 2022, is alive and well in Herefordshire, having recently been released by the Swedish forces after years of being mothballed in storage. It has only covered 4000km from new, is 12/24 volt and has a Bofors recoilless rifle "for use as a highly mobile anti-tank platform," according to the owner. Other Volvo military vehicles included the 1960s amphibious BV202 and extremely light L3304 anti-tank Howitzer carrier.

Other postwar military staff cars converted for military use include the rather ungainly looking four-wheel-drive TP21 dubbed the 'Sow,' a 1950s PV830 taxi based passenger vehicle used by the Swedish Defence Forces for three decades and based on commercial running gear.

Rear aspect of the same vehicle. It was based on the 4x4 C303, and only recently sold off by the Swedish Army.

APPENDIX 2 – KEY ACHIEVEMENTS IN MOTORSPORT

Volvos have certainly featured across many European races both in Europe and across the world. Following privately entered cars for a year or two, from 1958, the main factory-backed focus has certainly been on PV444, PV544 and then the Amazon. Factory car racing was withdrawn following a fatal accident in the 1960s, but resumed much later with the 240 Turbo (1985/6) and 850s (1994/5/6). The 850 saloon racers replaced the estates after just one season, brought on board following a change to aerodynamic and spoiler rules which would have made the estate uncompetitive. Both body types were displayed to a stunned audience fully kitted-out and liveried at the 1994 Stockholm Motor Show, with Tom Walkinshaw of TWR in attendance; he remained tight-lipped, stating a decision had yet to be made as to whether TWR would use saloon or estates on the forthcoming BTCC. The decision to race the load carriers came a few weeks later at the Geneva Motor Show.

Many other cars have been used for racing and rallying, entered by very keen, not to mention deep-pocketed, private individuals, which would warrant a book all on its own.

Some of those have made it into the list in this section.

Most of the media publicity in the past has been centred around the Singh brothers and their 1965 East African Safari win with a refurbished PV544, plus the pioneering Gunnar Andersson, who was adopted as a works Volvo driver mid-season in 1958! Tom Trana and later BTCC Richard Rydell feature a lot, too.

Below is a non-exhaustive list of some of the more notable achievements from 1945-1995 (to list every single entrant in a Volvo would have taken a lot of room). It is presented in model order.

Brothers Joginder and Jaswant Singh on the East African Safari in their 'secondhand' PV544 ...

Car	Event	Year	Position	Driver
PV444	Liège-Rome-Liège	1957	8th	Harris
PV444	Midnight Sun	1957	1st	Jansson brothers
PV444	Viking	1957	1st	Grondal/Bernsten
PV444	Viking	1957	2nd	Ingier/Floysvik
PV444	Acropolis	1958	3rd	Gunnar Andersson
PV444	Midnight Sun	1958	1st	Gunnar Andersson
PV444	Adriatic	1958	1st	Gunnar Andersson
PV444	Monte Carlo	1958	4th	Loffler/Johansen
PV444	Deutchland	1958	3rd	Gunnar Andersson
PV444	Tulip	1958	1st	Gunther Kolwes
PV444	Liège-Rome-Liège	1958	Excluded	Martensson
PV444	Viking	1958	1st	Ingier/Floysvik
PV444	Viking	1958	2nd	Andersen/Gjolberg

... the brothers came first overall in this gruelling 1965 event, which meant great short-term publicity as, alas, the car was to cease production shortly afterwards.

Car	Event	Year	Position	Driver
PV544	Thousand Lakes	1959	1st	Callbo/Nurmimaa
PV544	Thousand Lakes	1959	2nd	Ingier/Berntsen
PV544	Viking	1959	1st	Ingier/Berntsen
PV544	Viking	1959	3rd	Grondal/Solberg
PV544	German Rally	1960	1st	Gunnar Andersson
PV544	Midnight Sun	1960	3rd	Gunnar Andersson
PV544	Viking	1960	1st	Andersson/Karlsson
PV544	Tulip	1961	2nd in class	Gunnar Andersson
PV544	Liège-Sofia-Liège	1962	3rd	Jacques Patte
PV544	Acropolis	1961	2nd	Gunnar Andersson
PV544	Deutchland	1961	3rd	Gunnar Andersson
PV544	Monte Carlo	1962	6th	Gunnar Andersson
PV544	RAC	1963	1st	Tom Trana
PV544	RAC	1964	1st	Tom Trana
PV544	Monte Carlo	1964	6th	Tom Trana
PV544	Acropolis	1964	1st	Tom Trana

Car	Event	Year	Position	Driver
PV544	Midnight Sun	1964	1st	Tom Trana
PV544	1000 Lakes	1964	2nd	Tom Trana
PV544	Swedish	1965	1st	Tom Trana
PV544	East African Safari	1965	1st	Singh brothers
Amazon	Scottish	1959	6th	Neate
Amazon 122	Monte Carlo	1961	14th	Gunnar Andersson
Amazon 122	Liège-Rome-Liège	1962	2nd	Marang
Amazon 122	Tulip Rally	1962	2nd	Gunnar Andersson
Amazon 122	RAC Rally	1962	1st Class 4	Gunnar Andersson
Amazon 122	RAC Rally	1962	2nd Class 4	Sylvia Osterburg
Amazon 122	Liège-Sofia-Liège	1962	3rd	Patte/Rousselle
Amazon 122	Six Hours Race	1963	1st Class B	Tom Trana
Amazon 122	Midnight Sun	1963	1st Coupé des Dames	Sylvia Osterburg
Amazon 122	Polish	1963	2nd	Gunnar Andersson
Amazon 122	Acropolis	1963	2nd	Gunnar Andersson
Amazon 122	Monte Carlo	1963	8th	Olle Dahl
Amazon 122	Monte Carlo	1963	9th	Gunnar Andersson
Amazon 122	Acropolis	1963	3rd	Skogh/Berggren
Amazon 122	Geneva	1963	3rd	Gunnar Andersson
Amazon 122	Thousand Lakes	1963	2nd	Tom Trana
Amazon 122	Tulip Rally	1963	3rd	Gunnar Andersson
Amazon 122	Liège-Rome-Liège	1963	13th	Pilhatsch
Amazon 122	Liège-Rome-Liège	1963	15th	Gunnar Andersson
Amazon 122	Liège-Rome-Liège	1964	10th	Patte
Amazon 122	Liège-Rome-Liège	1964	17th	Pilhatsch
Amazon 122	Monte Carlo	1964	Class winner	Tom Trana
Amazon 122	Shell 4000 (Canada)	1964	1st	Klaus Ross/John Bird
Amazon 122	Shell 4000 (Canada)	1964	4th	Olivier Gendebien
Amazon 122	Acropolis	1965	1st	Skogh/Berggren
Amazon 122	Acropolis	1965	1st	Carl Skogh
Amazon 122	1000 Lakes	1966	2nd	Tom Trana
Amazon 122	KAK	1966	3rd	Tom Trana
Amazon 122	RAC	1966	3rd	Tom Trana
Amazon 122	Swedish Rally	1966	3rd	Tom Trana

Pictured with three on-board, car 281 was this 122S of Sven and Per Nystrom at the Stockholm start of the Monte Carlo Rally in 1959. It achieved 49th overall. That year nine Amazons, seven PV444s and five new PV544 cars were entered.

The 240 Turbo made a superb track car, winning the 1985 European Touring Car Championship.

Car	Event	Year	Position	Driver
Amazon 122	Marathon de la Route	1967	3rd	Christoffersson
Amazon 122	1000 Lakes	1967	3rd	Hannu Mikkola
Amazon 122	Scottish	1970	4th	Grewe
P1800	Liège-Rome-Liège	1961	Crashed	Gunnar Andersson
P1800	Midnight Sun	1961	Retired	Tom Trana
Daf	Liège-Rome-Liège	1963	19th	Ransy
Daf	Marathon de la Route	1967	6th	Brel
142	Donau-Castrol	1968	2nd	Poltinger/Morinsky
142	Scottish	1972	1st (Ladies award)	Heinonen
142	Welsh	1973	2nd	Walfridsson
142	Press on Regardless	1973	2nd	James Walker
142	RAC	1973	4th	Walfridsson
142	Thousand Lakes	1973	3rd	Markku Alen
343	European Rallycross	1977-80	Various	Per-Inge Walfriddson
240 Turbo	ETCC	1985	1st	Thomas Lindström/ Gianfranco Brancatelli
240 Turbo	ETCC	1986	Various results	Thomas Lindström/Johnny Cecotto

Car	Event	Year	Position	Driver
850 estate	BTCC	1994	Various results	Jan Lammers/Rickard Rydell
850 estate	ASTC	1996	Various (Australia)	Peter Brock/Tony Scott
050 saloon	BTCC	1995	Various results	Tim Harvey/Rickard Rydell
850 saloon	BTCC	1996	Various results	Kelvin Burt/Rickard Rydell

Note: the 850 was replaced by the S40R for the 1997 season.

The 1985 240 Turbo had 300hp on tap … It returned in 1986 for one more racing season.

The BTCC 850 estate certainly turned a few heads. Some track drivers, having just been overtaken, complained they could not see beyond the large Volvo's tailgate!

The front-wheel-drive 850 estate on a 1994 BTCC event. For the following two seasons, saloon 850s were used due to an aerodynamic regulation change that would make racing the estates unfavourable.

APPENDIX 3 – MAIN VOLVO TV & FILM APPEARANCES

Listed here are many notable appearances of Volvos in (mainly) English spoken films and TV shows. All worth a look out for on YouTube.com, DVD or other streaming platforms. As there are a lot of TV shows that use Volvos as their transport but may not feature too much, this list concentrates on those that make both a regular appearance and are a main part of the show, an example would be the mustard 265 GL in *Lovejoy*, series one.

PV444 – *Monica Z*
PV544 – *Max Dugan Returns, Mousehunt, The Frighteners*
PV Duett – *Snoken, Between the Lines, The Jezebels*
Amazon – *Peak Practice, The Royal, The Avengers* (S7, Ep28), *Man in a Suitcase, The Sure Thing*
1800/1800S – *The Saint, Man in a Suitcase, Bridge of Spies, Department S, The Baron*
1800ES – *The Protectors, Next of Kin, Act of Vengeance*
144 – *The Bees, Night On Earth, Puppet on a Chain, Alfred Hitchcock Presents, The Love Ban*
145 – *Grange Hill, Good Life, Survivors, Changing Habits, The Brood*
164 – *Mission Impossible* (TV series), *The Protectors*
66 – *Frits en Freddy* (1980)

340 – *Roger* (short movie), *Gallowglass, Kidnapping Mr Heineken, Byker Grove*
360 – *A Very British Coup, The Situation*
440 – *Het Rijexamen, Eden*
460 – *Moving Target, Comic Sans, Mang Lung*
480 – *Brookside*
240 – *A Touch of Frost, Vanished Without a Trace, Floodtide, The 40 Year Old Virgin, The Martins, Traffik, Dr Sleep, Grynch – My Volvo* (music video), *Jonathan Creek*
244 – *Detroit Rock City, The Cold Light of Day, Love My Way*
245 – *When Strangers Appear, Careless, Chain of Fools, King of California, Deja Vu*
262C – *Bellflower, Love Crimes*
264 – *Rage and Honor, II, CHiPs*
264 TE – *Familien Gyldenkal* (1975 and 1976)
265 – *Lovejoy S1, Xtro, Holding the Fort, The New Statesman*
740 – *Driver's Ed Mutiny, Luther, The Dead Outside, Kindergarten Cop*
760 – *Travelling Man, The Midnight Man, Delusion*
780 – *Black Out, Hunter*
850 – *Airbag, Collision, Keeping Mum*
940 – *Midnight in Saint Petersburg, Hell, Horrible Bosses, The Chief*
960 – *Crush, Unhinged, Zebra Crossing*

Ten years ahead of any James Bond activity for Roger Moore, the production company for ABC Films approached Jaguar requesting a loan of the then-new E-Type, considered to be the best sports car on the market, having

Roger Moore with either NUV647E or NUV648E whilst filming The Saint TV series in the late 1960s.

The old-style log book for the 1967 NUV648E P1800S, with Roger Moore's name recorded on it.

been launched just a few months prior. Jaguar declined. Volvo was then approached, and within a week supplied a white P1800, and the rest is history. There were 116 episodes of *The Saint*, and many featured the P1800, albeit one of four white examples used: originally 1962 77GYL and 71DXC (now finally in safe hands and beautifully restored), then January 1967 NUV647E and NUV648E; the latter has Roger Moore's name on the original log book, as he used it for his own transport. This car has recently been restored and is also in

safe hands. The famous ST1 plate (now on a Mercedes) was not part of the inventory. Interestingly, Leslie Charteris, who wrote the Simon Templar books, later drove a late season 144, which still exists and was recently auctioned. Ironically, when a revamped series returned in 1979 with Ian Ogilvy in the lead role, Jaguar finally jumped in on the act, with hero Simon Templar now driving a white XJ-S!

Some interesting UK appearances from 140 and 200 series estates exist in TV archives. Character Jerry Leadbetter drove a yellow 145 de luxe in *The Good Life*, whilst Abby Grant drove the same car, DJH180K, in BBC's *Survivors* a short while later, and it also appeared in *Grange Hill*. David Jason played a detective who regularly drove a tatty old blue 240 estate in earlier episodes of *A Touch of Frost* between 1992 and 2000, until it was finally destined for the TV (and real life) scrapyard. The car had false number plates from a Ford Transit, but there were fleeting glimpses of the correct A388JCK. And then there was the always tappety-sounding yellow 265 GLE SDY111S, regularly driven by Britain's favourite antique dealer Lovejoy until it was spectacularly rolled in the Suffolk countryside in a 1985 episode after the brakes were 'fixed.' The real vehicle survived and continued to be used for another five years … Look on youtube.com for a more spectacular rollover and explosion of a 264 in *Rage and Honor II*.

71DXC proudly displayed on a Volvo Enthusiasts' Club stand with associated signs, and cardboard cut-out of Roger Moore. (Courtesy Kevin Price, VEC)

Chrome quarterlight handles (P1800).

P1800 early door handle and chrome trim.

264 badge now proudly displays 'Fuel injection'.

Chrome hinges and finishing piece on late 240 estate.

Also from Veloce Publishing –

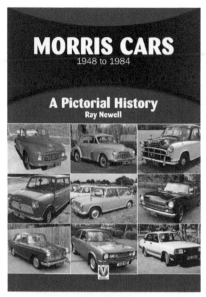

ISBN: 978-1-787110-55-7
Paperback • 21x14.8cm • 144 pages
• 425 colour pictures

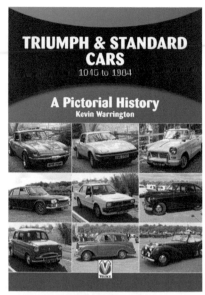

ISBN: 978-1-787110-77-9
Paperback • 21x14.8cm • 96 pages
• 244 colour pictures

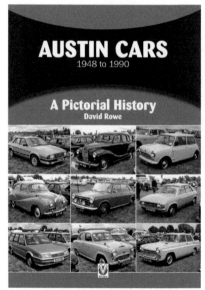

ISBN: 978-1-787112-19-3
Paperback • 21x14.8cm • 112 pages
• 275 colour and b&w pictures

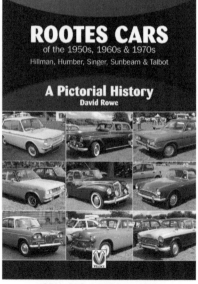

ISBN: 978-1-787114-43-2
Paperback • 21x14.8cm • 168 pages
• 1083 colour and b&w pictures

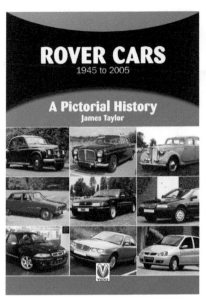

ISBN: 978-1-787116-09-2
Paperback • 21x14.8cm • 80 pages
• 300 pictures

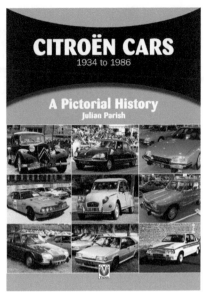

ISBN: 978-1-787116-36-8
Paperback • 21x14.8cm • 152 pages
• 350 pictures

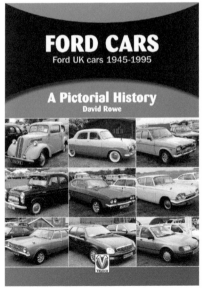

ISBN: 978-1-787116-42-9
Paperback • 21x14.8cm • 160 pages
• 330 pictures

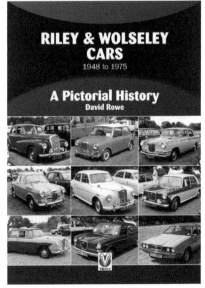

ISBN: 978-1-787117-91-4
Paperback • 21x14.8cm • 104 pages
• 352 colour and b&w pictures

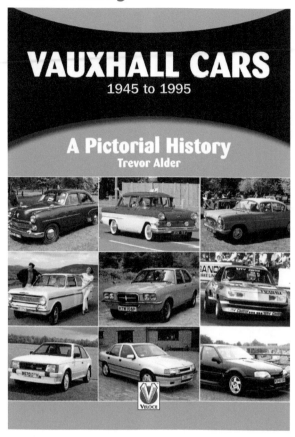

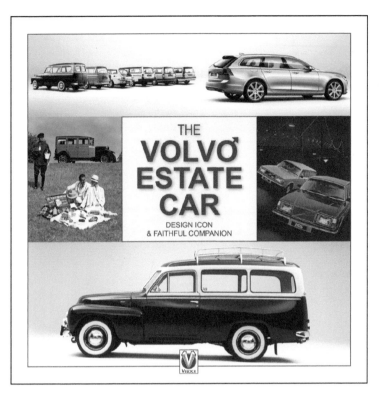

ISBN: 978-1-787116-07-8
Paperback • 20.7x20.7cm • 160 pages • 319 pictures

Now in paperback!
This book chronicles the history of the world's most iconic estate car (station wagon), with a wonderful variety of images, some of which have never been published before. The first Volvo car went on sale in 1927 and this book tells the story of the much-loved estate right up to the V90.

For more information and price details, visit our website at www.veloce.co.uk
• email: info@veloce.co.uk • Tel: +44(0)1305 260068

Index